THE OTHER INVISIBLE HAND

JULIAN LE GRAND

THE OTHER INVISIBLE HAND

Delivering Public Services through
Choice and Competition

PRINCETON UNIVERSITY PRESS
PRINCETON AND OXFORD

To the memory of my mother

Contents

Acknowledgements

Many people have helped me in writing this book and in the work on which it is based. I owe a significant intellectual debt to Alain Enthoven, whose early work on the British National Health Service inspired many of the reforms that are analysed here. Alain has kindly provided an afterword in which he points out the relevance of the book's analyses to US problems with public services and hence to an American audience. This has the additional benefit of showing how the book's arguments can be applied outside the British context and thereby enhancing their relevance to other countries.

Another person to whom I am much indebted is David Lipsey, one of the most respected critics of extending choice in the (British) public sector. Again he has generously given of his time to write an afterword, offering some thoughtful criticisms of some of the book's arguments. Although the provision of afterwords such as these is a little unusual, I hope that readers will find them interesting, enjoyable and useful complements to the main text.

Others from academia and elsewhere who have greatly helped my understanding of the issues involved include Nicholas Barr, Gwyn Bevan, Geoffrey Brennan, Simon Burgess, Harry Caton, Zachary Cooper, Anna Dixon, Keith Dowding, Jon Glasby, Howard Glennerster, Nicola Lacey, Tony Laurance, Damaris Le Grand, Carol Propper,

Anne West and David Willetts. Many of these people have provided helpful comments on various chapters or on the manuscript as a whole. I am grateful to David Chater and Alistair Pettigrew for allowing me to use material in chapter 5 from joint work that I have done with them. Ruth Robertson gave some valuable research assistance at a key point in the book. The editors of *Political Quarterly* allowed me to use material in chapter 6 which is also being published there. And I am greatly indebted to my editor at Princeton University Press, Richard Baggaley, for his support, including his gentle persistence in ensuring that the manuscript was finally completed.

I also need to thank the people with whom I worked in the mysterious institutions of government, from whom I learned an enormous amount. I am particularly grateful to Andrew Adonis, who originally arranged for me to work in the Policy Directorate at Number 10 and who has done more to initiate, to develop and to implement the Labour government's educational reforms, including those concerned with choice and competition, than any other single person. I am also very grateful to those with whom I worked in that remarkable environment, especially Simon Stevens, my predecessor as health adviser and an unparalleled source of expertise and wisdom on health services, and Paul Corrigan, one of my successors as health adviser; Ken Anderson, Nigel Crisp, Dominic Hardy, Simon Leary, Barry McCormick and Tim Wilson, all then at the Department of Health; Michael Barber and Adrian Masters, then at the Prime Minister's Delivery Unit; Will Cavendish and Peter Brant at the Prime Minister's Strategy Unit; the ministers with whom I worked, including John Reid and John Hutton; and last, but of course not least, a great prime minister, Tony Blair, who so generously gave me the opportunity to work with him on the radical programme of public service reform that he inspired and led so effectively.

Introduction

Ask people what they want from the public money that is spent on health care and education, and the answer will be simple: a good service. Sometimes they will add that they would like this service to be on their doorstep: a good, local service. A high-quality local school; a caring, responsive, family doctor; a top-class district hospital.

This short book is about how these aims can best be achieved. It examines four means of doing so: trust, where professionals, managers and others working in public services are trusted to deliver a high-quality service; targets and performance management, a version of what is often termed command-and-control, where those workers are instructed or in other ways directed to deliver a good service by a higher authority; voice, where users of public services communicate their views directly to service providers; and the 'invisible hand' of choice and competition, where users choose the service they want from those offered by competing providers.

The book does not argue for one of these means being used to deliver public services to the complete exclusion of the others. On the contrary, it contends that each has its merits, and that, in consequence, all have their place in the delivery of public services. But it does also point to the disadvantages of each system. And it pulls together evidence and theory to argue that, in most situations, services whose delivery systems incorporate substantial elements of choice and competition have the best prospect of delivering a good local service. Properly designed, such systems will deliver services that are of higher quality, more responsive and more efficient than ones that rely primarily upon trust, command-and-control or voice. Moreover—contrary to much popular and academic belief—they will also be more equitable, or socially just.

The book develops some of the arguments that I made in an earlier book, *Motivation, Agency and Public Policy*, to which it is in some ways a natural successor (Le Grand 2003). But it is also based on work that I did when working as a senior policy adviser to the prime minister at 10 Downing Street, where I was privileged to be seconded for two years.

My appointment to Number 10 meant that, as a kind reviewer of my previous book pointed out, I was having to put my money where my mouth was. The government of the then prime minister, Tony Blair, was putting into place public sector reforms of a kind that I had long advocated. So I was now in a position of having actually to defend these ideas in a political and policy arena. I also had to help put them into practice, and to confront the technical and political difficulties involved in policy implementation. I could no longer hide behind a veneer of academic detachment; I could not pass the difficult questions on to others to deal with; if a technical or political problem arose, I could not simply ignore it, but had to think of a way of dealing with it.

And it is that experience that has dictated both the content and the structure of this book. One of the criticisms of the reforms involving choice and competition that the Blair government was introducing, especially into

the National Health Service (NHS) and education systems, was that they were incoherent: a contradictory mish-
mash of ill thought out policy gimmicks with little basis
in theory or practice. In fact, the reforms stemmed from a
well-grounded understanding of the problems involved
in delivering public services and, in particular, the difficulties in delivering them through forms or models of service delivery that did *not* involve elements of choice and
competition—including trust, command-and-control and
voice. Hence it seems important to spell out these problems here; and that is the task of chapter 1. This discusses
the ends or aims of public services, and elaborates some
of the problems in achieving them through the means of
trust, command-and-control and voice.

Chapter 2 then develops the general arguments for
extending choice and competition in public services. And
it provides a response to some of the arguments levied
against the policies concerned, ones that I encountered
frequently during my period in government: that people
don't want choice, that choice is a middle class obsession,
and that choice threatens the public realm.

Another consequence of my working at Number 10 was
that, while it did not change my mind about the general
merits of the choice-and-competition model as a means of
delivering public services, it did sharpen my awareness of
some of the problems involved in putting it into practice.
And that has shaped chapters 3 and 4, which look at those
problems in the context of education and health care, and
offer some ways of resolving them.

Chapter 5 looks at some possible ways of going beyond
current policies and extending the basic ideas into areas
where they have rarely been tried. It concentrates on three
specific proposals, each of which develops one aspect of

the earlier discussions: patient budgets in health care, a disadvantage premium in education, and a new type of provider for the social care of children.

Finally, chapter 6 provides a brief overview of some of the politics associated with choice and competition. It looks at some of the positions on the issue that are often taken by key political or other interest groups, and discusses how the relevant arguments may be addressed. Again this derives in large part from my working in government, of which a key part was developing an understanding of the source of the objections to public service reform as an essential part of trying to deal with them.

One point about terminology. The expression 'public services' can mean many things, including its literal interpretation as services for the public. It is often taken to refer specifically to services that are of fundamental importance to the public, such as education, health care, social care, housing or transport. And it usually implies services for which there is some form of state or government intervention, whether in its finance, provision, regulation or all three.

Here I use the term in the sense of both fundamental importance and (one form of) state intervention. I consider primarily the services of health care and education, with some attention to social care. And I consider the parts of those services that are wholly or primarily financed by the state. The source of finance could be general taxation or some kind of hypothecated tax such as national or social insurance. The state may also provide some or all of a service, or regulate its provision; but these are not necessary conditions for it to be considered as a public service.

It is worth noting that many of the arguments made here can be applied to public services other than education, health care or social care. And some of them have reference to any service-delivery organization, whether publicly or privately financed.

The book is intended to appeal to as wide an audience as possible, and is written in what is, I hope, an accessible style. Jargon is avoided so far as possible. The references use the author–date abbreviated style, with full details provided in the bibliography. For those who wish to take the arguments further there is a brief section on further reading.

CHAPTER ONE
Ends and Means

As noted in the previous chapter, when considering publicly funded services such as health care and education, most people simply want a good service. But what exactly is a good service? And how do we get it? Put more precisely, what are the *ends* that we are trying to achieve with our public services and what are the *means* for achieving those ends? And what are the advantages and disadvantages of particular means for achieving particular ends? This chapter and the next address these questions in a general fashion, reserving more detailed discussion of the special (but important) cases of health care and education for later chapters.

Ends

There are many possible interpretations as to what constitutes a good public service, or, more generally, as to what are the ends or aims of public services. Indeed, arguably, one of the reasons why debates over the various means or models for delivering public services are so contentious is not because of disputes over the effectiveness or otherwise of those means in achieving particular ends, but because of differences over the desirability of the ends themselves.

However, I shall argue that there are at least five basic attributes, the possession of which would constitute a good public service. These are that the service should be of high *quality*; that it should be operated and managed *efficiently*; that it should be *responsive* to the needs and wants of users, while simultaneously being *accountable* to taxpayers; and, last, but not least, that it should be delivered *equitably*.

Quality

As with all the ends that we discuss in this chapter, there are many possible meanings of the term 'quality' in the context of public services. It could be defined in terms of the 'inputs' to those services, such as the number and type of the staff who work there: the level and degree of specialization of the medical professionals in a hospital, or the qualifications and experience of the teachers in a school. Other inputs could include the size and condition of the service's facilities: the number of hospital beds, a school's classroom sizes, the age of the relevant buildings. Second, quality could be interpreted in terms of the 'process' of service delivery, such as the courtesy or consideration with which users are treated, or the amount of time they have to wait for the service. Alternatively, it could be measured in terms of 'outputs' or the 'activities' undertaken in the process of delivering a service—such as the number of operations undertaken in a hospital or the numbers of children taking exams at a school. Finally, quality could be defined in terms of the 'outcomes' that result from using the service—such as the improvements in patients' health that result from medical treatment or the acquisition of skills such as numeracy, literacy and higher-level analytic skills that result from school attendance.

Of these possible interpretations of quality, the two most important for the actual users of public services are probably those concerned with process, especially the courtesy, consideration and speed with which they are treated, and those concerned with outcomes, especially health improvement and skills acquisition. Ironically, however, the two that are perhaps the most often used in practice are inputs and outputs—largely because they are the most easily measurable.[1] In fact, it is often difficult to disentangle all these elements, especially at a general level, and we shall not try to do so here. Suffice it to say that at different points in the debate over public service delivery each of them is likely to be important, and that in what follows we will try to make it clear which is being considered when.

Efficiency

Efficiency, often considered to be solely the preoccupation of mean-minded accountants and economists, tends to get a bad press in popular and academic debate. Worries about the money being spent on public services

[1]There is a particular problem with outcomes, in that it is often difficult to attribute a given outcome improvement (such as in the health of a patient) to a particular item of public service (such as a course of medical treatment). For the outcome may in large part be due to a variety of factors that are not within the control of the providers of the service concerned (such as the patient's own recuperative powers). This is one of the reasons why, although both providers and policy makers often pay lip service to the importance of outcomes, in practice they usually give more attention to factors that are more under the control of the service, such as inputs, processes and outputs.

are contrasted unfavourably with what are perceived to be the more legitimate concerns of the consequences of those services for individuals' and families' health, education or welfare. Oscar Wilde's definition of a cynic is indeed often applied to accountants and economists: people who know the price of everything and the value of nothing.[2]

However, properly defined, efficiency is an essential element of a good public service. For an efficient service is one that delivers the highest possible quality and quantity of that service from a given level of resources. Inefficient services, ones where resources are misused or wasted, are services that lower the overall levels of users' health, education or welfare compared with what they could have been. The real 'price' of a service is not the money that was spent on providing it: it is the other services that could have been provided had the money not been spent in that way. This is what economists call the 'opportunity cost' of the provision of a service: the opportunities that could have been exploited had the resources not been used for the service concerned.

So those who use the Wilde aphorism to criticize economists, accountants and others concerned about efficiency are misguided. For knowing the price of something does not mean knowing nothing about value. Indeed, it means just the opposite: it means knowing the value of what is forgone by paying that price, and comparing that value with the value of the service being bought. This is not as neat as Wilde. But such knowledge is essential if we are to obtain the highest quantity and quality of public services from the resources we put into them. For if we pay too

---

[2]The definition is from *Lady Windermere's Fan*, Act 3.

high a price—if we forgo things that are of a higher value than those we are actually receiving—we will be not be getting the best possible service, and people will suffer in consequence.

Responsiveness and Accountability

It might seem reasonably uncontroversial to assert that a good public service is one that is responsive to the needs and wants of its users. Indeed, responsiveness of this kind is arguably an essential element of what constitutes quality in public services; and the concept could be wrapped up under the general heading of quality and not considered separately, as it is here. However, a major criticism of public services in many countries has been their apparent inability to respond to their users. Hence it does seem desirable to give responsiveness a separate entry in the list of possible ends for those services.

In fact, responsiveness as an end can be given a more solid philosophical justification from what the philosopher Albert Weale has described as 'the principle of equal autonomy' (Weale 1983, p. 42).[3] This he formulates as

> all persons are entitled to respect as deliberative and purposive agents capable of formulating their own projects, and that as part of this respect there is a governmental obligation to bring into being or preserve the conditions in which this autonomy can be realized.

---

[3]The importance of this principle in this context was drawn to my attention by Rudolf Klein (see Klein (2005), reprinted in the 2006 paperback edition of Le Grand (2003)).

Being responsive to the needs and wants of users could be viewed as an essential element of according the respect to 'deliberative and purposive users'. To use a metaphor that I have employed elsewhere, the principle of autonomy requires that users are treated less like pawns, the weakest pieces on the chess board, and more like the most powerful piece, the queen (Le Grand 2003).

But there are some qualifications to this principle. Users of most public services of the kind we are considering here are not charged for them. Much education and health care is provided free at the point of use. Hence users do not actually face the price or opportunity cost of the services they consume. And it may sometimes be the case that the opportunity cost to the rest of the community from their use of that service is greater than the benefit to them that results from their use. In such cases, since society consists of both them and the rest of the community, there is a net loss to society as a whole.

Put another way, considerations of responsiveness or even the principle of autonomy cannot always dominate considerations of efficiency, especially in a world where people are not being charged for the services they use. For it may be that some users' wants are relatively trivial, and that resources can be better spent elsewhere meeting others' more urgent ones.

The issue of payment raises a further question. Should public services be not only responsive to the needs and wants of its users, who in most cases are not paying directly for the service, but also responsive to the needs and wants of those who *are* paying for it: the taxpayers? Responsiveness to taxpayers is often not described in these terms, but instead is expressed in the language of account-ability. So another way of putting this question is to ask to what extent should considerations of user responsiveness dominate those of taxpayer accountability?

Of course, almost by definition, most taxpayers will use 'universal' public services at some point in their lives; and most users of public services pay taxes, both directly through income tax and indirectly through VAT or excise taxes such as those on alcohol or tobacco. Hence the preferences of a state's citizens in their role as taxpayers are unlikely to be very different from their preferences in their role as users. In most cases, both taxpayers and users are likely to want services that are provided to a high standard, that are efficiently run, and that are responsive to the needs and wants of users.

But there may be occasions when the interests of user and taxpayer differ. Geographical or other forms of redistribution of resources in the name of equity may result in the taxpayers in one part of the country subsidizing public service users in another. Visitors to the country or recent immigrants may make use of public services while having paid relatively little in taxes. And these differences may in turn generate differences in preferences for service delivery between taxpayers and users that will not always be easy to integrate. In short, providing a public service is likely to encounter some tensions between meeting the requirements of user responsiveness and meeting those of taxpayer accountability.

Equity

Equity—or its close synonyms, social justice and fairness—is obviously a key element in any good public service. Indeed, for many people it is the reason why services such as health care and education are in the public domain at all. If, by virtue of their income, their social class, their gender or their ethnicity, some patients have preferential access to health care, or some parents have preferential access to education for their children, then this is widely regarded as unfair or inequitable. And no public service should be inequitable in that sense.

Again we have to add some qualifications. Elsewhere I have argued that differences in an individual's situation that arise from factors beyond that individual's control should be treated differently than those that arise from factors wholly or largely within his or her control. So, for instance, a wealthy individual who chooses to go and live in a remote rural area is not entitled to demand the same ease of access to medical services or schools as might prevail in the rest of the country—at least not on equity grounds.[4] But, overall, the notion that a good public service is one where there is broadly equal access for all, regardless of social or economic status or other differences irrelevant to their need for the service, is both important and relatively uncontroversial.

Trade-Offs

We saw in the discussion of user responsiveness and tax-payer accountability that it may not always be possible to meet all the requirements of both simultaneously. Much the same can be said of the other ends discussed here. In some cases and in some situations, there may have to be trade-offs between ends that have to be made in service delivery. So, for instance, it may not be possible—in fact,

[4]See Le Grand (1984, 1991) for a full development of this argument.

it almost certainly will not be possible—to provide equal access for everyone to the highest quality of service in the country. As we have seen, services that are fully responsive to the needs and wants of some individuals may not be very efficient in terms of the interests of the wider community. Equity or fair treatment for public service workers may not always coincide with the requirement for services that are responsive to the need and wants of users. And so on.

The notion that there may be a trade-off between ends is one that many people outside the policy world often find difficult to recognize. This is partly because such ends have moral values attached to them, and the idea of trading-off different types of moral claims against each another is one that is neither easy to grasp nor to accept. However, such trade-offs are an ineluctable fact of policy formation and development, and have to be acknowledged as such. No public service will successfully meet all these different ends; and hence no means of public service delivery will be perfect. But there are other reasons, too, why means of service delivery may not be perfect. And to these we now turn.

Means

Fundamentally, there are four means or 'models' for delivering public services to attain the ends spelt out in the previous section. There are models that rely upon *trust*: where professionals and others who work in public services are simply trusted to deliver a good service, with no interference from the government or from anyone else. Then there are models that use *command-and-control* (also known as hierarchy), where the state, or an agency of the state, engages in service delivery though a managerial hierarchy in which senior managers give orders or instructions concerning delivery to subordinates. A version of this is known as *targets and performance management*; this has been widely used in recent years, especially in Britain, and it will form the focus of our discussion here, summarized under the heading of targets. Next are models that rely upon *voice*, where users try to get a good service by communicating their views directly to providers in a variety of ways, from face-to-face contact with professionals through to complaints to elected representatives. Finally, there are models that depend upon user *choice*, with or without *competition*, whereby users can choose from a variety of different providers who may compete with one another for custom.

In what follows we examine the merits and demerits of these models. In this chapter we consider trust, command-and-control and voice; in the next chapter, choice and competition. One final point before we do this. In practice, virtually all systems of public service delivery use some combination of all of the models, and, as we shall see, there is good reason for this. In consequence, the debate about which model is 'best' is not about replacing one in its entirety by another in its entirety. Instead, it concerns the desirability of shifting the balance in a delivery system in the direction of one model or another, but without completely displacing the remaining ones. However, it is useful to distinguish conceptually between the four models for our purposes here. For each has its own advantages and disadvantages, and it is much easier to see these if the models are considered in relative isolation from one another.

Trust

The basic idea behind the trust model is simple. The government sets the overall budget for the service; those who provide the service spend it as they wish. The providers are usually professionals of one kind or another—doctors, nurses, teachers, head teachers, social workers—and, in spending the budget, these professionals are trusted to do so, in a word, professionally. That is, they are presumed to allocate resources in such a way as to achieve the aims of a good service: a service that is efficient, responsive, accountable, equitable and of high quality.

Under the trust model, professionals and others in public services are often assumed to work in collaboration with one another, either informally or through more formal networks. Hence it is sometimes known as a 'network' or collaborative model. However, the trust model is in fact rather broader than this; for it relies upon trusting professionals in all situations whether they are working collaboratively in networks or not.

This model has many advantages as a means of delivering public services. For obvious reasons, the people working in the services themselves like it, especially the professionals. The latter's training encourages them to think of themselves as independent and autonomous, working in environments with little in the way of managerial hierarchy, and with few people telling them what to do. They have the freedom to organize their lives as they want to and to deliver the service in whatever fashion they think appropriate; and it is a freedom that, understandably, they relish.

It also has advantages from the point of view of policy makers, and indeed from that of service users. The relatively high morale of professionals under the model can make them more productive. Further, as we shall see, a major problem with some of the other models is that they are likely to require some form of monitoring of the quality of the service being provided, monitoring that has to be done either by the government or by the users themselves. Quality in many areas of public services is difficult to assess, especially if it is defined in terms of outcomes. So effective monitoring, if it is possible at all, can be very costly in terms of resources, as well as being demoralizing and demotivating for those on the receiving end of the process. Any model that can apparently avoid the need for such monitoring is therefore likely to be more productive than ones that cannot, other things being equal. And, in a broader moral sense, a system that seems to trust the people who work within it is more attractive, and even perhaps more admirable, than one that engages in continuous monitoring and heavy supervision of those who work within it.

Moreover, if quality is difficult to monitor, so is another of our ends of public services: efficiency. For, in the absence of good information about quality, it becomes difficult to decide whether a low-cost service is efficient, or is simply one that is delivering low quality. Simply trusting service providers to deliver is an economical way of avoiding these difficulties.

But can providers be trusted to deliver? Only so long as a crucial assumption about the *motivation* of professionals is fulfilled. Specifically, they have to be motivated primarily by a concern for the welfare of those they are serving, and not by their own material self-interest. Put another way, the model assumes that all those who work in public services are altruistic 'knights', rather than self-interested 'knaves'. Their only concern is to meet the needs and wants of the service user along with those of the wider community; their only interest that of promoting social welfare. Hence they can be trusted to deliver quality services in an efficient, responsive, accountable and equitable fashion.

The terminology of knights and knaves stems from a previous book of mine, which made extensive use of that metaphor (Le Grand 2003). The term 'knave' comes from the works of the eighteenth-century philosophers David Hume and Bernard Mandeville, who used it to describe an individual whose only concern is with his or her private self-interest. In that book, I contrasted this with the 'knight', an individual whose principal concern is with the welfare of others. So knightly doctors, teachers or social workers would be ones who put the needs and wants of their patients, pupils or clients above their own; whereas knavish professionals are those who prioritize their own immediate interests above those of the people they were supposed to serve.

Knightly behaviour could derive from a number of sources. It could derive from what one might term 'pure' or 'act-irrelevant' altruism: distress at the suffering of others and a desire to see that suffering relieved, regardless of who actually performs the act of relief. Or it could come from what I have termed elsewhere 'act-relevant' altruism, where there is distress at others' suffering, but also a desire to undertake the acts of relief oneself—preferably involving some degree of personal sacrifice (Le Grand 2003, chapters 2 and 4). Or indeed it may not be motivated by any form of altruism but by more selfish concerns, such as a boost to one's professional esteem or a desire to seek the approbation of others.[5]

Whatever its source, reliance upon knightly behaviour is an essential element of the trust model. But what if some of those who work in public services are somewhat less than perfect knights? In that case, the trust model encounters problems. For the pursuit of self-interest in the trust-model context is likely to result in a service that is organized more in the interests of its providers than in those of its users. Surgery opening hours, the timing of appointments, the length and structure of the school day, and, more fundamentally, the medical treatments offered, the school curricula taught—all are likely to be affected, and not in a way that benefits users.

In fact, a review of the available literature on the motivation of those who work in the public sector suggests, not that they are either exclusively knights or knaves, but, as with most people, a mixture of the two (Le Grand 2003, chapter 2). It also seems that which kind of motivation is to the fore at any one point in time often depends on circumstances. Inevitably, therefore, sometimes those circumstances are such that knavish behaviour is encouraged— with damaging consequences for the delivery of services.

Moreover, even if public service professionals were always perfect knights, there can be problems about relying upon knightly motivations. First, knights are not

[5]There is an obvious question here as to whether behaviour driven by these kinds of more self-centred concerns can be described as knightly or altruistic. Indeed, there is a broader question as to whether any form of behaviour can be driven by true altruism, in that even when people behave altruistically they are presumably doing it because they want to and it is therefore serving some interest of theirs. Resolution of this issue is beyond our purview here; I discuss it more in Le Grand (2003, pp. 27, 28).

always motivated to be very efficient. Doing some good, not necessarily the maximum good, is often sufficient motivation. This can also get in the way of innovation: it is easier to keep on doing what one has always been doing so long as some good is being done than it is to make the necessary changes to implement new ways of doing things. And, in the absence of comparative performance measures, they may not be aware how mediocre their service is.

Second, knights may have their own agenda. They may be altruists in the sense that they have concern for the welfare of others, but their interpretation of what would contribute to that welfare may differ from the government's view (an example might be faith schools) or indeed that of the users themselves.

Third, providers may be knaves from the point of view of government, in that they subvert policy, but knights from the point of view of users, in that they bend rules in the latter's favour. In fact this could be part of a wider pro-trust argument: knights may be favoured by users because they act as user advocates in the face of a possibly uncaring bureaucracy. But this assumes that some parts of the system—the uncaring bureaucracy—cannot be trusted, which casts doubt on the viability of the whole model.

But here a point made by the policy analyst Rudolf Klein has relevance.

> Knightly behaviour may be the problem rather than the solution. ... [F]rom the perspective of users, knights may be authoritarian paternalists acting in the sure faith that they are altruists who know best. If the pursuit of self-interest at the expense of the public

interest is the pathology of knavery, self-righteous rectitude is the pathology of knighthood.

Klein (2005, p. 94)

Put another way, knightly advocates operating within bureaucratic systems may fundamentally be paternalists: giving users what the knights think users need, but not necessarily what users think they need.

And knights' perceptions of the needs of the wider community may be limited. When faced with individual distress, knights find it difficult to recognize limits to resources. This is perfectly understandable: who would like to be in the position of a doctor having to tell the patient in front of her that she cannot have a possibly life-saving drug on the grounds that the money could be more effectively spent elsewhere? And yet if it could be more effectively spent elsewhere, it should be.

The operation of the trust model in a network context raises further problems. For it requires that the members of the network trust each other. Network members must be sure that other members are not pushing their own self-interest or the interests of the institution for which they work (Mayer et al. 1995; Tomkins 2001). They must also have faith in all the members' capabilities: in their efficiency and ability to undertake the tasks with which they are entrusted.

Unfortunately, these conditions may not always be fulfilled. An interesting illustration of this is provided by a recent study of a Scottish health care cooperative (Hannah et al. 2006). Following devolution in 1997, Scotland deliberately moved away from a choice-and-competition model for health service delivery towards one based on trust and networks. The health care cooperative studied

involved both GPs and health service managers and was
intended to improve primary health care services in Scotland. Unfortunately, GPs fundamentally mistrusted the
health managers, doubting their capability, their benev-
olence and their integrity. In consequence there was little improvement in services. The networks, of which this
cooperative was one, were eventually abolished.

Moreover, it is difficult to see how, if the operation
of the trust model does not work, the model could be
improved while staying within its essential requirement:
that of trusting the service provider. It might be possible
to encourage more knightly behaviour by, for instance,
encouraging professional peers to assess and review
performance; but this is appealing to a non-altruistic
motivation—a desire to please one's peers—and comes
close to being a knavish incentive structure.

Further, peer pressure is subject to norms that may be
more a reflection of the collective interests of the profession concerned than of the individual interest of the user.
Thus it may be exercised to defend existing ways of doing
things, salaries or job conditions.

As we shall see, the nature of most public services is
such that any system of service delivery will have to rely
upon a measure of trust in the people who deliver it.
But, overall, both intuition and experience tell us that sole
reliance upon the trust model is unlikely to achieve our
aim of a good service. What is needed is a system that com-
bines elements of the trust model of service delivery with
other models in such a way that the existence of both knavish and knightly motivations are acknowledged, and that
knightly motivations are preserved but directed toward
serving the wider interest.

Targets

Our next model, a version of what is commonly termed command-and-control, is almost the complete opposite of trust. Here, professionals, and indeed all those who work in the service concerned, are part of a management hierarchy, whereby senior managers instruct subordinates in service delivery.

Command-and-control can take on a variety of forms. A version of it that has been widely implemented by the British government recently is what we might term 'targets and performance management'. This sets targets of various kinds, usually numerical ones, for public sector organizations such as schools or hospitals to achieve, and then offers rewards or penalties to the staff of those organizations for achieving or failing to achieve the target. The rewards could be greater autonomy for the organization and/or financial bonuses or promotion for the staff. The penalties could involve greater outside intervention in the running of the organization and demotion or the sack for the staff. The penalties could also include so-called 'naming and shaming': the publicizing to peers or the general public of poor performance with the intention of humiliating the staff or organization concerned and hence encouraging them to do better.

Now the British experience suggests that this kind of performance management has a major advantage for a model of public service delivery. It works—at least in the short term. The NHS in England has adopted a wide variety of targets coupled with heavy performance management: what has been described as a 'regime of targets and terror' (Bevan and Hood, forthcoming).

In consequence, some key aspects of service delivery (notably patient waiting times) have sharply improved. For instance, in 2002, around a fifth of all those arriving at accident and emergency departments were still waiting to be seen four hours later. A target was set that 98% of accident and emergency attendees should be treated, discharged or admitted to hospital within four hours of their arrival. By 2005 this target had been achieved—and this despite an increase of over 25% in the number of people attending accident and emergency departments in that period (Department of Health 2005a, Statistical Supplement).

Targeting the numbers of patients waiting for elective surgery had a similar impact. In 1999 more than a quarter of the relevant patients in England were waiting longer than six months for surgery, and over 4% for more than a year. Key targets were set and performance management was introduced. By 2005, there was no one waiting longer than a year and only 5% waiting longer than six months (Bevan and Hood 2006, p. 420, table 1).

The English ambulance service provides another example. In 2000, among the services for which comparable data are available, only one ambulance trust was able to meet at least 75% of category A calls (ones that involve life-threatening emergencies) within eight minutes. In 2002, this—responding to 75% of category A calls within eight minutes—was set as a key target. By 2005, more than four-fifths of these trusts were meeting the target, and even the worst performer was managing over 70% (Department of Health 2005a, Statistical Supplement).

The United Kingdom has recently devolved powers concerning the delivery of public services policy to each of its constituent countries; England, Scotland, Wales and

Northern Ireland. Following this devolution in the late 1990s, the three countries other than England all adopted rather different models of public service delivery, especially in health. This is rather convenient; for it provides a natural experiment with which to compare the performance of different models.

Take Wales, for instance. On receiving its devolved powers over health policy, the Welsh Assembly abolished targets and refused to allow its officials to use top-down performance management, concentrating instead on promoting cooperative working between health, local government and the voluntary sector. Basically, it decided to rely upon the trust model for delivering services, with its leaders explicitly rejecting the English model as not suitable for Wales.

As policy analysts Gwyn Bevan and Christopher Hood have shown, the results for Wales lend little support to the effectiveness of the trust model. There was a substantial increase in waiting lists. In 1999 11% of patients waited longer than a year for elective surgery; by 2003 it was up to 16%. Ambulance response rates to category A calls within eight minutes were around 50% in 2001; they were still 50% in 2004 (Bevan and Hood 2006). And this was despite the fact that Wales had more resources per head than England and a similar rate of growth in those resources (Alvarez-Rosete et al. 2005).

Economists Katherina Hauck and Andrew Street have compared the performances of hospitals on either side of the England–Wales border over a six-year period before and after devolution. They showed that the English hospitals had increased levels of activity, undertook proportionately more day-case activity and had declining mortality rates. At the same time, activity levels remained constant in Wales, the proportion of day cases fell and mortality rates rose. English patients waited less time and were more likely to be treated within the target waiting period. All this they attributed to the 'stronger performance management regime' in England than in Wales (Hauck and Street, forthcoming).

The Auditor General for Wales agreed. He criticized the system for providing neither strong incentives nor sanctions to improve waiting time performance. Indeed the system was perceived as having actually rewarded organizations that failed to deliver on waiting times by giving them extra resources (Auditor General for Wales 2005).

It is worth noting that all of this began to change in 2003. Wales began to introduce performance management, and some patient choice. In direct consequence, waiting lists fell.

Targets and performance management have also appeared to work in English education. In particular, numeracy and literacy have sharply improved in English primary schools. The percentage of eleven year olds achieving level 4 or above in English rose from 57% in 1995–96 to 79% in 2006, and that achieving level 4 in mathematics rose from 54% in 1995–96 to 76% in 2006.[6] There have also been improvements in GCSE results taken at the end of compulsory education. The percentage of pupils aged fifteen at the beginning of the academic year who achieved five or more GCSE examination passes at grades A* to C increased from 45% in 1997 to 56% in 2005, an increase of

[6]Statistical Bulletin of the Department for Education and Skills: National Curriculum Assessments for seven, eleven and fourteen year olds, various years.

eleven percentage points in absolute terms (Department for Education and Skills 2001, 2006b).[7]

It has to be noted that some of these improvements (especially in English and mathematics) seem to have been achieved not so much because of the setting of targets in the area (although targets were set), but rather because of the straightforward command-and-control imposition of a compulsory numeracy and literacy teaching hour on schools. A systematic study of the imposition of a literacy hour on some English primary schools before it was made compulsory found large increases in attainment in reading and English in pupils exposed to the literacy hour compared with pupils who were not. Interestingly, boys received a greater benefit than girls (Machin and McNally 2004).

So forms of command-and-control, including targets and performance management, can raise standards. If there is a well-defined objective (reducing waiting times, improving numeracy and literacy) and if the process involves a fairly heavy-handed application of rewards and punishments, then it appears as though this model can achieve at least some of the components of what constitutes a good public service.

The fact that some forms of command-and-control can work, at least in the short term, should not be too surprising. After all, many of these techniques are used to good effect by large organizations outside the public sector. However, there are reasons to believe that the command-and-control model does present problems for delivering

[7]There has been much discussion as to whether the increase reflects a genuine improvement in standards: see, for instance, West and Pennell (2003).

public services in the longer term. Some of these are generic to the model wherever it is applied, but others are more specific to the kinds of public service with which we are dealing.

To see some of the generic problems, consider those that may be associated with the setting of targets. First, they discourage continuous innovation and improvement; once the target is achieved there is no incentive to go further. Second, targets can lead to 'gaming'. Gaming can take a variety of forms: it can range from a straightforward fiddling of the figures to more subtle changes of behaviour that mean that the target is attained but that also lead to undesirable long-term consequences.

An example of gaming with behaviour change would be the unnecessary admitting of patients into a general hospital ward from the accident and emergency department in order to count them as 'seen' within the four hours. Bevan and Hood cite other examples, including an ophthalmology service that met a target for new outpatient appointments by cancelling and delaying follow-up appointments (which were not targeted); in consequence, at least twenty-five patients were estimated to have lost their vision over two years (Bevan and Hood 2006, p. 421).

Third, since missing targets can happen for reasons beyond managerial control, the penalties that come with missing the targets (or indeed the rewards that accompany hitting them) can seem arbitrary and unfair.

There are ways of making targets work better. To avoid any arbitrariness involved in hitting or missing targets, they could be tied only to factors that are entirely within managerial control. To reduce the risk of gaming, Bevan and Hood have suggested that an element of uncertainty could be introduced as to exactly what was being targeted. So the targets could be retrospective, or they could change from year to year. Bevan and Hood have also argued for an independent body to assess data quality so as to reduce figure manipulation.

However, none of these changes would affect the central problem of targets and performance management, and indeed of all forms of command-and-control, in the public sector. This is the effect on the motivation and morale of providers. There is nothing as effective at demotivating and demoralizing providers as a ceaseless bombardment of instructions from above. And this is even more pronounced in public services, where a large proportion of those involved are professionals used to a high degree of autonomy in their workplaces. Few people like being told what to do; but this is especially so for doctors, nurses, teachers, social workers and other professionals. For they are trained to believe that they are independent decision makers who have the principal responsibility for those they are providing a service for, and that they should not be subject to the whims of bureaucrats or politicians.

A related point concerns the fact that targets are a statement of priorities. What is targeted is assumed by the policy makers who set them to be of more importance than that which is not. However, the people who have to meet the target may not share these priorities; in their judgement, as the phrase goes, the service may hit the target but miss the point. In such circumstances, although they may nonetheless conform to the requirements of meeting the targets, they are likely to do it at best unhappily and at worst resentfully.

Performance management and other forms of command-and-control have their place in the short term. For they can be used to overcome entrenched resistance to change, and to show that what was previously thought impossible can nonetheless be achieved. But they are not a long-term solution to the problems of public service reform.

What is preferable instead is a system with incentives for reform *embedded within it*. Providers will then endeavour to provide a high-quality service without having to be told to by politicians or by managers acting for politicians. And these incentives should include a bottom-up element. If responsiveness is to be achieved, and the principle of autonomy fulfilled, users' perceptions of their needs and wants should not be treated as irrelevant in determining what those needs and wants are—as unfortunately they can be in both trust and target models.

Voice

One model for running a bottom-up public service is that of 'voice'. Perhaps the best definition of voice is that of the man who originated the term in this context, Albert Hirschman. He defined it as any attempt to

> change, rather than to escape from, an objectionable state of affairs, whether through individual or collective petition to the management directly in charge, through appeal to a higher authority with the intention of forcing a change in management, or through the various types of actions and protests, including those that are meant to mobilize public opinion.
>
> Hirschman (1970, p. 30)

Put another way, voice is shorthand for all the ways in which users can express their dissatisfaction (or indeed their satisfaction) by some form of direct communication with providers. This could be through informally talking to them face-to-face: parents talking to teachers about the education of their child, patients chatting to their GP. It could be more indirect: talking to parent governors of a school, even becoming a parent governor, speaking at a patient or public consultative forum, joining the board of a hospital. It could be more formal: invoking a complaints procedure, complaining to elected representatives, invoking the ombudsman, and so on. And it could be collective, through the process of voting.

Now the voice model has its advantages as a means of public service delivery. Obviously it takes direct account of users' needs and wants, at least as they themselves perceive them. Moreover, individual voice mechanisms, especially, can be rich in useful information. Telling providers what is wrong with the service they provide (and indeed what is right with it) can be very helpful to providers who want to improve—indeed, much more so than simply not turning up for appointments or, as with the choice model, just switching to another provider.

Collective voice mechanisms have the advantage that they are indeed collective: that they take account of the interests of the community. On the other hand, they are clumsy instruments for dealing with the kind of individual decisions with which we are concerned here. Parents who are dissatisfied with their local school, or patients with their local hospital, can vote for local elected representatives who are promising to provide better ones; but, for their votes to be effective, a number of conditions have to be fulfilled. There has to be an election in the offing; their views have to be shared by a majority of other voters; the issues concerning the quality of schools or hospitals have to be the principal factors affecting the election; politicians promising better schools or hospitals have to be among the candidates; and, if these politicians are elected, they have to have some effective method for ensuring school or hospital improvement. It is rare that all of these conditions will be met.

Further, despite their collective nature, these mechanisms are often poor at dealing with inefficiency or underperformance. Voters are rarely faced with the costs of meeting their service requirements. When they are not faced with those costs, they can simply vote to increase or maintain services at other people's expense. Indeed, this often happens when school or hospital closure proposals are put to a vote; the voters concerned usually do not have to bear the costs of keeping the institutions concerned open, and in consequence usually vote the closure proposals down. And there may be equity consequences: a majority can also vote to segregate a minority, excluding them by formal or informal means from the service concerned.

More individualistic voice mechanisms, such as complaints procedures, also have their problems. They require energy and commitment to activate; they take a good deal of time to operate; and they create defensiveness and distress among those complained against. Users who complain are not necessarily those who have the most to complain about; and adversarial relations between professionals and users, especially tied to a threat of lawsuits as they may well be, can lead to expensive and inefficient defensive reactions on the part of providers.

More fundamentally, many individualistic voice mechanisms favour the educated and articulate. The better off have louder voices: they also have better contacts and sharper elbows. And they are adept at using their voices to demand access to more extensive services (such as specialist outpatient consultations, diagnostic tests, inpatient treatments, better teachers and so on). Generally, middle class patients and parents are more articulate, more confident and more persistent than their poorer equivalents. Moreover, the medical practitioners and the school principals who are taking the relevant decisions are more likely to speak the same kind of language, and thus relate better to middle class patients and parents.

In addition, many of the middle classes have friends or acquaintances who are in one of the relevant professions, and who can help them navigate the system. Hence the middle classes are much better placed than those lower down the social scale to ensure that they get quality medical treatment for themselves and their families and better education for their children. Further, they are more likely to participate in the institutions of voice: becoming a parent governor of a school, for instance, or a member of a hospital board.

Moreover, the middle classes do not always have to rely upon voice to get their way. Even in systems where there is no public system of choice, there are nonetheless two possibilities for exercising a form of choice. First, in most countries, there is always the possibility of opting out (or never entering) the public system: using the individual's or the family's own funds to buy private education or private health care (Canada, where private health care is outlawed in some provinces, is a partial exception, although even there, there is the possibility of crossing the border).

Second, there is the possibility of moving house so as to benefit from good schools or hospitals. That this is a real issue is illustrated by a number of studies in the United

Kingdom. A recent study by the nation's biggest mortgage lender, the Halifax, found that houses are valued at 12% more than the regional average if they are located in the same areas as the most successful secondary schools, confirming an earlier, similar report by another large mortgage lender, Nationwide (*The Guardian*, 26 March 2005, p. 23). Gibbons and Machin found that a 10% improvement in league table performance for primary schools can be expected to add 3% to the price of a house located close to the school; it is a very local effect, one that halves 600 metres away from the school gate. In London and the South East the result can be that moving from an area with weak primary schools to an area with stronger ones can cost an average of £61,000 and on occasion very much more than that. (Interestingly, they also found that because of confusion over admissions and lack of clear information about school performance, parents exhibited a 'herd' mentality, going for schools that were difficult to get into, not necessarily those that were top performing (Gibbons and Machin 2005).)

It is not surprising that in these circumstances non-choice systems can favour the better off. For instance, a recent review of utilization of the British NHS found that:

- The unemployed, individuals with low incomes and those with poor educational qualifications use health services less relative to need than the employed, the rich and the better educated.

- Intervention rates of coronary artery bypass grafts or angiography following heart attack were 30% lower in the lowest socio-economic groups than in the highest.

- There were 20% fewer hip replacements among lower socio-economic groups compared with higher ones despite 30% greater need.

- Social classes IV and V had 10% fewer preventive consultations than social classes I and II after standardizing for other determinants.

- A one-point move down a seven-point deprivation scale resulted in GPs spending 3.4% less time with the individual concerned (Dixon et al., forthcoming).

But even this middle class bias is not the principal difficulty with voice. That lies in the absence of incentives. On their own, voice mechanisms do not provide much by way of incentives for improvement. If a provider has a monopoly on the supply of a service, it can ignore the complaints of its users with relative impunity.

This can be partly resolved by coupling voice with one of the other models. For instance, voice could be coupled with trust, and rely upon the knightly motivations of providers to rectify any deficiency that is brought to their attention by users. The snag with this is that, as we have seen, not all public service providers are knights, and, even when they are, they are not always sympathetic to pushy users.

Alternatively, voice could be coupled with command-and-control. Providers that ignored complaints could be subject to sanction from above. However, this would suffer from the problems of demoralization and demotivation already mentioned in connection with command-and-control. Providers being told how to behave are not likely to be the most willing to offer a responsive service.

Or it could be coupled with choice. If providers know that ultimately the dissatisfied can exit—can go elsewhere—they really have an incentive to improve. Choice can give power to voice. But, to see this properly, we need to examine choice in more detail. That will be the task of the next chapter.

Conclusion

No system of public service delivery can or should dispense entirely with targets (or command-and-control, more generally), voice or trust. Targets and performance management can break down institutional resistance to change, especially in the short term. Voice gives important information to providers about the quality of the service they are providing. Many public services have processes and outcomes that are difficult for users, governments or even managers properly to monitor quality and cost; so trusting providers to deliver quality and efficiency in these areas is unavoidable.

However, all these models had a central problem that made it difficult to rely upon any one of them as the principal basis for delivering good public services: that of the absence of the right incentives for providers. Thus the trust model offers little in the way of direct incentives of any kind. Instead, it relies upon all providers being motivated to provide a good service exclusively by (a rather specific form of) knightly motivation, a phenomenon that, although not impossible to find, is not likely to be sufficiently widespread for a whole system of service delivery successfully to be based upon it. Knightly behaviour could be encouraged by the introduction of various mechanisms such as peer review, but these can fall foul of collective self-interest with unsatisfactory consequences for service delivery.

The various versions of command-and-control, including targets and performance management, do offer direct incentives, but of a kind that are sometimes crude, often punitive and almost invariably demotivating and demoralizing for those on the receiving end—with damaging consequences for the quality of service they are prepared to provide. In consequence, while the model might work to achieve simple targets in the shorter term, it does not provide a longer-term solution for the problem of public service delivery. And voice models, while having the merit of directly taking into account the views of users, again offer little on their own by way of incentives for providers to improve their service—unless they are combined with elements of trust or command-and-control, in which case they suffer from the problems associated with those models. Moreover, they tend to favour the better off.

In short, if the aim is to achieve a good service—a high-quality service that is run efficiently, responsive to the needs and wants of users, accountable to taxpayers, and equitable in its treatment of users and workers—we need to look elsewhere.

CHAPTER TWO
Choice and Competition

The previous chapter analysed some of the advantages and disadvantages of three ways of, or models for, delivering public services: trust; targets, performance management, and other forms of command-and-control; and voice, both individual and collective. We concluded that all have their place in any system of public services, and indeed that it would be difficult to imagine a system that did not have some of these elements within it. However, we also argued that each of them had considerable problems as a sole, or even principal, model for public service delivery; and, if the aim of obtaining a good public service was to be achieved, that it would be necessary to consider some alternative.

In this and subsequent chapters, we consider just such an alternative: choice and competition. We argue that models that rely significantly upon user choice coupled with provider competition generally offer a better structure of incentives to providers than the others we have discussed, and, as a result, are more likely to deliver high-quality services efficiently, equitably and in a responsive fashion. To adopt Adam Smith's famous metaphor, usually applied to private markets, the government can use the 'invisible hand' of choice and competition to achieve its aims in public services (Smith 1776/1964, book IV, chapter 2, p. 400).

The argument is not exactly uncontroversial, and the second half of the chapter is concerned with an examination of the three most commonly voiced (and indeed perhaps the most fundamental) criticisms of the model: that 'people don't want choice, they want a good local service'; that choice is a 'middle class obsession'; and that it 'threatens the public domain'. These do not by any means exhaust the possible problems associated with the model's implementation. But the others tend to be more context specific, and so we address these in the subsequent chapters dealing with health care and education.

The Meaning of Choice and Competition

First, some terminology. There are a variety of different kinds of choice that users can make in the context of public services: where, who, what, when and how. There is choice of provider (where): that is, choice of hospital, choice of general (or primary care) practice, choice of other medical facilities, choice of school. Then there is choice of professional (who): choice of general or family practitioner, choice of hospital specialist or consultant, choice of other medical practitioners, such as practice nurses or physiotherapists, choice of teacher. There is choice of service (what): choice between different forms of medical treatment, such as drug regimes or types of surgery, or, in education, choice of curriculum or forms of pedagogy. Then there is choice of time (when): choice of appointment time, choice of time for day-case surgery or choice of time to go into a hospital as an inpatient. Finally, there is choice of access channel or method of communication (how): generally face-to-face in most public services, but increasingly through the phone or the Web. The principle of 'choice' in public services includes decisions on all these dimensions.

The decisions are not necessarily independent. Patients may choose a particular medical provider because of its opening hours or shorter waiting times, because they want to see a particular professional, or because of the specialist treatment they offer. In education, a parent may choose a particular school for a child because of the type of curriculum (e.g. specialist school) or style of pedagogy (e.g. Montessori) it offers. Some providers may offer different forms of access, such as phone consultations, and be preferred for that reason. However, it is useful to keep the distinctions between the different kinds of choice in mind, because the arguments for and against extending choice can vary according to which type of choice is being considered.

It is also important to distinguish who is doing the choosing. This could be the users themselves, relatives of the users (such as parents for schools), individual agents for the users (such as GPs choosing on behalf of their patients) or collective agents choosing on behalf of users (such as local authorities awarding contracts to suppliers on behalf of users).

This chapter and the next two chapters concentrate primarily on choice of provider (such as schools, hospitals) by users and/or their families. They emphasize choice in relation to providers, because that is where much of the policy and political debate is centred, and because, as noted above, that decision often incorporates the others. And they concentrate on choice by users (or the immediate agent of a user, such as a parent choosing a child's school), partly for similar reasons and partly because collective choice raises a set of issues that are rather different from user choice and that are beyond our purview here.

Competition is relatively easy to define. It is simply the presence in the public service of a number of providers, each of which, for one reason or another, are motivated to attract users of the particular service. This is to be contrasted with a unitary or monopoly service, where there is only one provider that has to be used by everyone who wishes to receive the service.

Another term that appears in what follows is 'quasi-market'. A quasi-market is like a market in the sense that there are independent providers competing for custom within it. But it differs from a normal market in at least one key way. This is that users do not come to a quasi-market with their own resources to purchase goods and services, as with a normal market. Instead the services are paid for by the state, but with the money following users' choices through the form of a voucher, an earmarked budget or a funding formula. The quasi-market is thus a fundamentally egalitarian device, enabling public services to be delivered in such a way as to avoid most of the inequalities that arise in normal markets from differences in people's purchasing power.[1]

There are various kinds of provider that can compete with one another in a quasi-market. These include small businesses, partnerships, workers' cooperatives, corporations, non-profit or voluntary organizations and publicly owned institutions. So introducing competition and quasi-markets into public services should not be confused

[1]See Le Grand and Bartlett (1993) for further discussion of the term 'quasi-markets' and of their nature.

with the so-called privatization of those services, although it often has been in some debates over the issue (see, for example, Pollock 2005). For it is perfectly possible to have competition between publicly owned or non-profit entities without any participation from the private sector. It is the presence of competition that matters, not the ownership structure of providers; for, as we shall see in a subsequent chapter, the kind of behaviour induced by competition is rather similar, regardless of the type of provider.

Choice and Competition: The Model

There are three principal arguments in favour of choice and competition as a model for public service delivery. It fulfils the principle of autonomy, and promotes responsiveness to users' needs and wants; it provides incentives for providers to provide both higher quality and greater efficiency; and it is likely to be more equitable than the alternatives.

First, the principle of autonomy. It will be recalled that, as formulated by Albert Weale, this 'asserts that all persons are entitled to respect as deliberative and purposive agents capable of formulating their own projects'. Offering a choice of provider of public services is part of that entitlement to respect.

To see this, and to see why the respect is itself desirable, consider your situation as a sick patient or a school pupil. When you are ill, you have few alternatives to seeking some form of medical treatment. When you are young, the state forces you to go to school. It is quite easy to imagine that you find yourself in a situation where you believe that the teacher or the doctor is incompetent or that he or she has taken a dislike to you (or an unwanted 'like' in some cases). Such a situation gives plenty of scope for petty tyranny and induced servility. And, even in the absence of any overtly bad conduct, the possibility for a student or patient to be miserable or frustrated because they are under the control of someone they do not like is far from inconceivable. Thus some capacity to choose alternatives is intrinsically desirable.

However, choice, especially when coupled with competition, has an instrumental value as well as an intrinsic one. For it provides incentives for providers to offer a higher quality service efficiently and in a responsive fashion. If providers face adverse consequences from not being chosen—if, for instance, they will lose resources if they cannot attract users—then they will want to improve the quality of the service they provide. In the examples above, suppose the unresponsive doctor or incompetent teacher knows that, unless they alter their behaviour, they will lose patients or pupils to other, more responsive practices or schools, and in consequence their livelihoods will be threatened. Then they will have a strong incentive to change their ways. Similarly, hospitals, practices and schools that do provide a good service (at least in the eyes of their users) will be encouraged to continue to do so, and indeed to improve further—especially if their erstwhile poor competitors are also having to improve their quality and efficiency if they wish to stay in the service.

Contrast this with the situation where there is no choice; where patients are compelled to go to the only hospital in their area, or children to the only school. Then, if they feel they are getting a bad service, the only mechanism they have for improvement is through exercising their voice: complaining to the service providers themselves or to the higher authorities. In the previous chapter we have seen some of the problems with this as a mechanism for improving the service they receive. It favours the articulate and confident, and thus contributes to inequity through privileging the better off. And, on its own, it provides little incentive for improvement—unless it is coupled with elements of the command-and-control model, which brings its own problems.

Now suppose another school or hospital opens in the area. Suddenly those who are dissatisfied with the local provider have somewhere else to go. The poor, the unconfident, the inarticulate no longer have to rely upon their (in)ability to manipulate the professionals and bureaucracy of the sole provider; they can now simply go elsewhere. Moreover, the local provider will know that. It will know too that, unless it listens to the complaints and does something about them, there will be a price to pay: it will lose its users and the resources that go with them. It will thus have a strong incentive to deal with the problems raised by users *whether or not* they exercise their opportunity to choose. The opportunity of choice will have given power to voice.

It is worth noting that this incentive structure will work whether providers are knaves, knights or a combination of both. Knavish providers will want to attract users because their livelihoods and thus self-interest depends on their staying in business. But knightly ones will also want to stay in business so that they can continue to provide a service of benefit to users. So they too will want to provide services that attract users.

One final point before we turn to some of the problems with the argument. It is important to note that, for the incentive part of the model to work, it is necessary to have both user choice and provider competition. It is possible to have one without the other: choice without competition and competition without choice. But neither on their own will achieve the ends set out above.

Offering choice on its own will achieve the illusion of user empowerment but is unlikely to deliver the reality. Consider an example of choice without competition: the British NHS prior to 1991. Then, GPs, acting as agents for their patients in need of specialist treatment, were able to refer them to any hospital in the country. However, hospitals that accepted patients referred in this way did not receive any extra funds for so doing, and thus did not have any direct incentive to attract patients. Indeed, if anything, their incentive was the reverse; since any extra patient involved extra work and there was no compensation for that work, the incentive was to delay admission by putting prospective patients on a waiting list or to try to shift them to other providers. This was not the best way to provide a high-quality service.

Provider competition on its own without user choice presents a different set of problems. There may be an incentive to improve in one sense, but not necessarily in the way that users want. For instance, staff rewards within hospitals and universities often reflect factors such as research output or peer approbation, considerations that may not relate to their quality as a doctor or teacher, at least as perceived by users. Also, the incentives are arguably less powerful than those offered by user choice. Nothing focuses the mind more effectively than the prospect of no one using your service.

So the model for the delivery of public services that relies upon user choice coupled with provider competition can deliver greater user autonomy, higher service quality, greater efficiency, greater responsiveness and greater equity than the alternatives. However, the word 'can' is important here. For this model can deliver these desirable outcomes in some situations, but not in all. In fact, there are many problems that choice-and-competition models face, and, in consequence, many conditions that have to be met before they will work as smoothly as the above suggests.

In fact, whether the choice-and-competition model actually delivers the aims of public services (or, at least, comes closer to achieving those aims than the alternatives) depends on the conditions under which it is used, and on the various policy instruments involved being properly designed. These in turn depend in large part on the nature of the service concerned; so they are considered in the subsequent chapters in the context of health care and education.

But there are three commonly voiced objections to the choice-and-competition model: objections that are less technical and less context specific than the conditions for success that will be discussed in the following chapters, but that, perhaps for that reason, are much more fundamental. They are that people 'don't want choice', that choice is 'a middle class obsession', and that choice and competition 'threaten the public domain'.

People Don't Want Choice

It is frequently asserted—often by those who have a good deal of choice in their lives already—that users of public services do not in fact want choice. This statement about the essential irrelevance of choice is often contrasted with what is claimed to be a preference for better quality, often phrased as 'people don't want choice, they want a good local service'. For example, the centre-left think tank, the Fabian Society, says the following about school choice.

> In some cases personal well-being could even be enhanced by the elimination of the need to choose and by the security of participating in a choice set of universal one-size-fits-all provision. For example, how many parents would prefer to send their children to the local school, with no choice in the matter, knowing that the education on offer met a national standard of high quality, rather than plunge into the positional competition known as parental choice which so often means parental fate for those unable to move their children in reach of 'good schools'?
>
> Levett et al. (2003, p. 55)

This argument has been bolstered by a recent publication by a US academic, Barry Schwartz: *The Paradox of Choice.* He argues—and indeed demonstrates through behavioural experiments—that, at least where the consumption of consumer goods is concerned, consumers frequently find excessive choice unsatisfying and demotivating (Schwartz 2004). He and other critics of choice have also pointed out that choice offers the opportunity of regret: and the more choice that is on offer, the more likelihood there is that the particular choice you make will result in regret.

Now it is true that, if people are offered the alternative of a good local service and a choice of service, they are likely to prioritize the quality of the service. So, for instance, a survey by the British Consumer Association's magazine *Which?* found that people 'value access and quality' more than choice in pensions, health services and education (*Which?* 2005, p. 7).[2] However, a moment's reflection will reveal that asking people to rank quality over choice is a nonsense. If you were offered a perfect television set or a choice of televisions, of course you would pick the perfect television. A quality service is not an alternative to choice; rather, choice is one of the possible means of obtaining a quality service. The question should not be, 'Do you prefer quality over choice?', but rather, 'Do you think a good-quality service will best be delivered by a system where you have choice, or by one where you have none?'

Schwartz is right to draw attention to the problems associated with too much choice. However, one cannot leap from an acknowledgment of these problems to the assertion that people do not want choice at all. In fact, if people are asked sensible questions about choices in public services—especially where they are starting from a situation where there is little or no choice (the system that prevailed in many British public services until relatively recently)—they do value it.

Take, for example, a poll undertaken by YouGov for *The Economist* on choice in both health and education that sampled 2,250 British voters in 2004 (*The Economist*, 7 April 2004). The study found that 76% of those with children in state schools consider it very important or fairly important that they have more choice over which schools their children attend, while 66% considered it important that they have more choice over the hospital that treated them.

---

[2]Irritatingly, very few details are given of this survey, including the questions asked or the numbers answering different questions.

Interestingly, with respect to health care in particular, over half thought that giving more control to patients was of greater importance for the NHS than giving it more money.

And this was not a freak result. A survey by the opinion research company MORI (now Ipsos MORI) in 2003 for Birmingham and the Black Country Strategic Health Authority found that 77% of people would like to make their own choice of hospital[3] Another MORI survey interviewed 1,208 members of the general public in August/September 2003, asking what would best represent their feelings if a GP had decided they needed treatment and offered them a choice of hospital both in the local area and in the rest of the country: 15% said they would like to make the decision themselves and 62% said they would like to make the decision but would need advice and guidance to help them decide (Page 2004). And yet another MORI survey of 1,016 adults in 2005 found that 60% of respondents thought that having more choice of health services outside of hospital would make services better; just 4% thought it would make them worse (Pfizer/MORI Health Choice Index 2005).

And we do not have to rely simply upon surveys of what people say they want. There is also evidence as to what people actually do if offered choice. A few years ago, the British NHS conducted a series of so-called 'choice pilots'. These were experiments offering patients who had been waiting longer than six months for certain kinds of elective surgery—principally cardiac surgery and removal of cataracts—a choice of an alternative hospital. In each case patients were offered a choice of up to three or four

[3]See www.ipsos-mori.com/polls/2005/pdf/bbcsha-public.pdf.

hospitals for treatment; in some cases they were assisted in making the choice by a specially appointed 'patient care adviser'.

The pilots were systematically evaluated (Coulter et al. 2005; Dawson et al. 2004). They proved popular. Take-up was high: 67% of patients offered a choice in London took up the offer to be treated at an alternative hospital more quickly, 75% in Manchester and 50% in the cardiac scheme throughout the country.

Generally, they generated a high degree of patient satisfaction with the processes and the outcomes. Representative comments included

- 'the patient choice idea is brilliant when it means that the operation is available much sooner—definitely to be recommended'; and

- 'I think the patient choice initiative scheme is an excellent one—I hope it will continue and that other people will be able to benefit from the scheme as I have done'.

Focus group and in-depth interview work confirms this view about the general popularity of choice. Research commissioned by the Department of Health from the National Consumer Council found interviewees who felt very strongly that they were entitled to a choice in health care.

As soon as you walk through the doctor's door, I don't see why you shouldn't have choice right from the beginning. I don't mean decisions, I mean choices.

Female with mild mental health problem, 45–54

If I am not getting help from somewhere, if one doctor is not helping, then I can go to another one of
my choice. That is why choice is important—I can go
somewhere faster and speedier and get something
done.

Asian male, 50+

So there are people who do want choice. But is it only
some people—especially, as many believe, the better off?

Choice Is a Middle Class Obsession

Results from the authoritative British Social Attitudes
Survey concerning peoples' attitudes to choice address
another common assertion of the critics of choice and competition: that, in the words of a prominent Labour politi-
cian opposed to the government's policies in this area,
'choice is an obsession of the suburban middle classes'.[4]

Overall, the British Social Attitudes Survey showed a
similar picture to the surveys already mentioned. Asked
whether patients should have choice of treatment, hospital
and outpatient appointment time, 65% of those surveyed
thought that patients should have a great deal or quite a
lot of choice of treatment, 63% said the same of hospital
choice and 53% of appointment time.

But this study also broke down the results by gender, social class, income and education. And these results
many will find quite unexpected. For they show that,
while there were majorities in each group that wanted

[4]'[C]hoice is an obsession of the suburban middle classes. But
when some families choose, the rest accept what is left. And the rest
are always the disadvantaged and dispossessed.' Roy Hattersley,
'Agitators will inherit the earth', *The Guardian*, 17 November 2003.

choice, the majorities were larger in the groups that were less powerful or less well off. So 69% of women wanted choice of hospital, compared with 56% of men; that 67% of the routine and semi-routine working class wanted choice, compared with 59% of the managerial and professional class; that 70% of those earning less than £10,000 p.a. wanted choice, but only 59% of those earning more than £50,000; and, finally, 69% of those with no educational qualifications wanted choice, compared with 56% of those with a higher-education qualification (Appleby and Alvarez-Rosete 2005).

This preference by the less well off for choice is not confined to health. The Audit Commission found exactly the same when it surveyed people's reactions to more choice for local government services. More specifically, the commission found that those in favour of choice were 'the least privileged, women and those who lived in the North and Midlands' (Audit Commission 2004, Summary).

These kinds of results—sustained majorities for choice, especially among the disadvantaged—are not confined to Britain. The Joint Center for Political and Economic Studies in the United States conducted a National Opinion Poll in 1999 on support for education vouchers and school choice. It found that, nationwide, 52% of parents, and 59% of public-school parents, supported school choice. However, the proportions were higher when minorities were considered: 60% of minorities supported vouchers while 87% of black parents aged 26–35 and 66.4% of blacks aged 18–25 supported vouchers (Bositis 1999).

Similarly, a study in New Zealand found that 96% of parents indicated they would like to select the school their child goes to, 80% of parents agreed that education should be funded in a way that enables parents to afford to send their children to the school of their choice, and that a higher proportion of parents with an annual income of $30,000 or less strongly agreed with the last statement than parents with an annual income of over $30,000 (Thomas and Oates 2005).

Additionally, an investigation of the political orientation of young adults (18–30) in Helsinki, Finland found that more of those with lower educational levels wanted choice in public services, more competition between the public and private producers of services and, in general, more private participation in the production and delivery of basic services (Martikainen and Frediksson 2006, pp. 53–55, 105, 106).

As we have seen, it is not true that the poor do not want choices. But this might not be sufficient to assuage the critics; for they could argue that even if the poor say they want more choice, if choice is offered to them in practice they will not take it up—at least not to the same extent as the more assertive middle classes (see, for example, Appleby et al. 2003). However, there is also evidence that the poor will actually take up choices if offered at least as much as the better off. The evaluation of the NHS choice pilots undertaken by the Picker Institute found no significant differences in the take-up of choice between the social groups either defined in terms of gender, educational status, household income or ethnic group: all were 65% or more. The only difference the evaluation did find was between the employed and unemployed, with, unsurprisingly, more of the former, 73%, willing to take up choice than the latter, 63% (Coulter et al. 2005). A study of the Greater Manchester Choice project produced similar results, concluding that 'there does not appear to be a significant difference in the acceptance of alternative providers [by patients] associated with ethnic background, gender or the IMD (Indices of Multiple Deprivation) of a patient's area of residence' (Joseph et al. 2006, p. 5).

So, in general, it is the poor, the dispossessed and the disadvantaged who want choice *more* than the allegedly rabidly pro-choice middle classes. As the Audit Commission (2004, Summary) puts it, 'it is precisely those groups, that many think will be less able to benefit from choice, who want it most'.

Nor, on reflection, should this be surprising. For, as we have seen in the previous chapter, the middle classes do well out of no-choice systems. With their loud voices and sharp elbows, and with their ability to move house if necessary, the better off get more hospital care relative to need, more preventive care and better schools. This is a point to which we return below.

Choice and the Public Domain

There is an intellectual tradition that reacts strongly against the arguments in favour of using choice and competition as a model for delivering public services. Members of that tradition are uncomfortable with the choice policies of governments (right or left) and with the arguments of others who advocate choice in that context, especially when it is coupled with terms such as competition and quasi-markets. For them, it indicates that the government concerned and its advisers have an obsession with consumerism and indeed capitalism, an obsession bent on turning public sector providers into little more than profit-driven supermarkets. And consumerism (and supermarkets), along with rampant capitalism, are to be abhorred.

The presumption underlying this argument seems to be something like this. Public service providers are not like supermarkets, especially when you consider those who work in them and their responsibility to users. In fact, those working in the public sector incorporate values of altruism and social justice—in contrast to those in the private sector, who are driven by a ruthless search for profit. In other words, the public sector is run by knights, the private sector by knaves. The introduction of choice and competition, especially if the latter comes from the private sector, will thus inevitably lead to the driving out of altruism or the public service ethos. The knaves will replace the knights. Hospitals and schools will become simply supermarkets peddling the latest fashion in education and health care.

Put more elegantly, choice, competition, and related terms like quasi-market, provider and consumer, are not—or should not be—in the public realm or domain. In the words of David Marquand:

> [T]he language of buyer and seller, producer and consumer does not belong in the public domain; nor do the relationships which this language implies. People are consumers only in the market domain; in the public domain they are citizens. Attempts to force these relationships into a market mould undermine the service ethic, which is the true guarantor of quality in the public domain. In doing so they impoverish the entire society.
>
> Marquand (2004, p. 135)

There are echoes here of the arguments of one of the original architects of the welfare state, Richard Titmuss. He argued as follows.

> The private market in blood, in profit-making hospitals, operating theatres, laboratories and in other sectors of social life limits the answers and narrows the choices for all men—whatever freedom it may bestow, for a time, on some men to live as they like. It is the responsibility of the state, acting sometimes through the processes we call 'social policy', to reduce or eliminate or control the forces of market coercions which place men in situations in which they have less freedom or little freedom to make moral choices, and to behave altruistically if they so will.

He went on:

> If it is accepted that man has a sociological and biological need to help then to deny him opportunities to express the need is to deny him the freedom to enter into gift relationships.
>
> Titmuss (1997, pp. 310, 311)

Another, related, form of critique is to use traditional economic theories concerning market failure to evaluate the idea of extending choice and competition in the public sector. For instance, David Lipsey, an adviser to the 1970s Labour government, and currently a Labour member of the House of Lords, in a significant article entitled 'Too Much Choice', draws attention to three characteristics of public services that make them different from the type of commodities sold in supermarkets, and thus inappropriate for the introduction of choice and competition: they generate 'externalities' (that is, they benefit people other than the immediate user) and they have agency and information problems for users (Lipsey 2005).

Poor user information is a genuine problem for choice in health care and education—although no more so than for other methods of giving power to users of those services, including their ability to exercise 'voice'—and we will address it in more detail when considering those services in subsequent chapters. However, the other economic arguments are more doubtful, especially when they are directed at these services. Most health care does not generate externalities, and the forms of health care that do, such as vaccination against infectious diseases, are best dealt with, not by denying patients choice of hospital, but by providing the care free at the point of use—a principle that indeed underlies most quasi-market systems of health care. Education externalities are best addressed again not by denying parents a choice of school, but by compulsory school attendance and a national curriculum. So far as agency (the fact that agents act on behalf of users instead of users acting themselves) is concerned, many argue that this is a particular problem for education, where parents make choices on behalf of their children. However, we do not use this as a reason to prevent middle class parents choosing private schools for their children; and it is not clear why we should use it to justify denying the less well off the power to choose between state schools.

Lipsey's article is in fact a balanced critique of choice, and he does not rule out extending user choice in some circumstances. But in some ways the interest of the article lies not so much in the details of the arguments used, important as those are, but in its tone. For, as with Marquand and Titmuss, this is broadly critical of applying the philosophy of market thinking to the public sector, which it claims involves adopting an 'analogy [that] is flawed'.

So is this kind of thinking necessarily corrosive of the 'service ethic' and does it undermine the public domain? The first point to note is that there are areas of the public domain where quasi-markets operate and where the consequences do not seem to be as dire as Marquand and others predict. British universities, for example, operate with state funding and under competitive pressure; so does the BBC. Although both universities and the BBC have their problems, they do not seem completely to lack the service ethic. In fact, from a variety of perspectives they are probably among the most successful of British public services; far from 'impoverishing the entire society', in many people's eyes they significantly enrich it.[5]

Further, there are already substantial areas of quasi-market operation within the 'public domains' of health care and school education, many of which have been there for a long time. Since the founding of the British NHS, GPs and dentists have operated as private businesses contracted to the NHS. Pharmacists and opticians, all private businesses operating in competitive markets, provide NHS-funded services and have done so since 1948. Many mental health services are provided by private-sector operators. In education, so-called voluntary aided schools are owned by the governing body or a charitable foundation, and the governing body is the legal employer. And much ancillary 'education', such as that for music, sport or driving, is privately provided. If all these have

[5]See Diamond (2006) for an interesting discussion of why the BBC is so relatively successful.

undermined the public domain, they have been doing so for a long time.

Part of the worry expressed by, especially, Titmuss in this area concerns the impact of the introduction of market-type incentives on the motivation of professionals. Put simply, the fear is that professional altruism will be driven out and replaced by crude self-interest: that the public sector knights will be turned into private-sector knaves. There is evidence on this question that I have reviewed in some detail elsewhere, and will not repeat here (Le Grand 2003, chapter 4). Suffice it to say that, although there were some studies that did indeed show a displacement of altruism by self-interest when market-type incentives were introduced where previously there were none, there were others that did not. Indeed, in one case, that of female voluntary carers, the introduction of market-type payments actually appeared to reinforce the caring motivations of the individual concerned. Generally, this research, coupled with the fact that some elements of the public service ethos still seem to remain in the quasi-markets mentioned in the previous two paragraphs, despite their longevity, suggests that the worry concerning its possible demise may at least be exaggerated, and at most be quite misplaced.

Finally, there is the question of the users themselves. If they are not allowed to act as consumers in the public domain, exercising the right to exit from a provider if they are dissatisfied with the service they are getting and to choose another, then how are they supposed to act? The answer may be as 'citizens': but this begs the question as to how a citizen should act.

In fact there are only two possible options for citizens faced with a bad public service, if choice is denied them.

One is passively to accept the bad service—to be 'pawns', as we discussed in a previous chapter, or 'service paupers', as Robert Pinker has described those who face unitary welfare monopolies (Pinker 1971, p. 142; see also Pinker 2006). The other is to express their 'voice', either individually or collectively. I suspect that this is the option that those who use the language of citizenship would prefer; but, as we have seen, it is a model of dubious effectiveness, and one that those at the lower end of the social scale find difficult to use successfully. So, in this world, the public domain is one where services are provided by knights, but where users are a combination of working class pawns and middle class activists with loud voices and sharp elbows: not the most attractive of visions.

In fact, the view that public services are staffed by helpful, welcoming knights is not one necessarily held by the public. When asked by MORI what words they thought applied to public services in Britain today, the highest ranked adjectives were (in descending order) bureaucratic, infuriating, faceless, hardworking (a positive note there), unresponsive and unaccountable. The lowest ranked were friendly, efficient, honest and open (MORI 2005).

Nor is the public afraid of the knaves in the private sector. When MORI told people in the Black Country that the NHS was now going to pay for patients to have their operations in private hospitals and asked them whether they were happy about this, 71% said they were, compared with just 11% who said they were unhappy. This is not very surprising, since in general they viewed the local private hospitals as of higher quality than the NHS ones.[6]

---

[6]See www.ipsos-mori.com/polls/2005/pdf/bbcsha-public.pdf.

The idea that the private sector provides better services than the public sector applies more generally than simply to health in the Black Country. When the British Social Attitudes Survey asked people whether government or business were better at providing a good-quality service, 51% said a private company, compared with 41% for government. And when asked whether private companies or government were better at running services cost effectively, 55% preferred private companies, compared with 39% for government (Appleby and Alvarez-Rosete 2005).

Understandably, the area in which people did prefer government over private companies in the British Social Attitudes Survey was on the ability to direct services where they were needed most. This is presumably because they saw private companies following normal private markets in favouring the better off. But quasi-markets do not suffer from this problem; indeed, as we shall see in subsequent chapters, the funding policies under the choice-and-competition reforms can be designed to encourage providers to meet the needs of the less well off, and even to specialize in doing so.

Conclusion

In this chapter I hope to have shown that a combination of choice and competition can provide the right incentives for providers to deliver a responsive service of high quality—a service that respects its users and that is produced in an efficient and equitable fashion. I have also argued that contrasting people wanting choice with people wanting a good local service is a false dichotomy; that in fact people do want choice; that choice may be the way to get a good local service; that, far from being a middle class obsession, the less well off want choice more than the middle classes; and that choice and competition can enhance, not destroy, the public domain.

The truth is that the public domain has no monopoly on virtue, the private sector no monopoly on vice. Public institutions are not run only by knights; private firms are not run only by knaves. Users are not pawns, but autonomous individuals who have the right to both voice and choice. The key is to understand the complexity of individual motivations and to design incentive systems accordingly. That will be the task of the next chapters in the context of education and health care.

CHAPTER THREE

School Education

Education systems around the world have been experimenting with extending parental choice in school education. In Britain, since 1989 parents have in principle had the right to send their child to any state school of their choice, subject to there being spaces available. Sweden introduced parental choice between state schools and publicly funded independent schools in 1992. New Zealand has offered some parental choice of school since 1989. In the United States, there have been extensive experiments in recent years with various education voucher schemes. And Belgium and Holland have long had parental choice of school, with funding following the choices made.

But increasing parental choice in education remains highly controversial. Critics of the policy allege that choice leads to unhealthy competition between schools, damaging educational standards; and that it is inequitable and divisive for communities, encouraging polarization and segregation by class, race and religion. Its advocates argue that, on the contrary, competition drives up quality and responsiveness; that choice does well in terms of community mixing compared with alternative systems of pupil allocation, such as those based on already-segregated residential catchment areas; and, through giving greater power to the less advantaged members of the community, it will also promote greater equity.

In this chapter we address some of these issues. We begin with a brief discussion of the ends or aims of educational policy. We then briefly review the international evidence on the impact of choice and competition in school education, and draw on that evidence and on theory to bring out the major lessons for choice-and-competition policy if it is successfully to meet those ends.

Ends and Means

As we noted in chapter 1, assessment of the desirability of a particular policy or policy reform has to give some account of the overall ends or aims of that policy. In fact, the potential ends of a publicly funded school education system are legion; but, as with the other services we have discussed, it is likely that in most countries at most times they can be summarized under the headings of quality, efficiency, equity, and responsiveness. However, there is also another aim that is more specific to school education: that of social inclusiveness.

Raising the overall quality of a school system is perhaps the principal objective of any such educational policy. But, as we saw in chapter 1, quality is far from unproblematic as a concept. It could refer to the 'inputs' into the system: the teachers, the school buildings, the classroom equipment. Alternatively, it could refer to the system 'throughputs' or 'process' factors, such as the satisfaction that pupils and parents derive from the actual school experience and/or the number of pupils taking national exams. Or, and this is the most common usage, it could mean the system's 'outcomes', such as the performance in national exams, or more general indicators of the skills and knowledge acquired by pupils and students as a result of their attendance at schools. Yet more ambitiously, the concept of quality could also refer to the overall impact of the system on the economy and on wider society: the contribution of school education to the training of the work force, to labour productivity, to citizens' understanding of social and cultural values and to enhancing their creative potential.

In practice, most empirical attention is usually focused either on educational inputs, or on one, relatively narrow interpretation of outcomes: the standards of educational achievement as measured by the results of examinations or other types of test. Inevitably, therefore, it is on these that we shall concentrate in this chapter. It should be noted, however, that they may only be a partial representation of the overall quality of a school system.

As with other services, efficiency is often identified with simple cost-cutting, and as such can be widely resisted in education circles, especially professional ones. However, a more sophisticated approach accepts that the quality of the education provided cannot be the only interest of an education system and that the way in which educational resources (or inputs) are used is also important. For, if resources are wasted, poorer outcomes will be achieved than if the resources had been used efficiently. Other things being equal, a high-quality, low-cost education is to be preferred to one that obtains similar quality but at a higher cost.

To achieve greater responsiveness to parents', pupils' and students' expressed wants and needs is, or should be, an end or aim of most school systems. As noted earlier, this can be justified by reference to Albert Weale's principle of autonomy: that 'all persons are entitled to respect as deliberative and purposive agents capable of formulating their own projects'. Such respect is an important element of any publicly funded service, partly because it is desirable in and of itself, but also because it is essential to maintain public support for the system. Nothing is more likely to drive parents out of the public sector than encountering professional arrogance or bureaucratic obstructionism in their dealings with it.

As with quality, equity in education is a much contested term. Variously it has been taken to refer to equality of opportunity, equality of access and equality of outcome. A common interpretation of equality of opportunity or equality of access (often used almost synonymously) is that the quality and quantity of education a child receives should depend only upon his or her ability to benefit from that education. That is, the education a child receives should be independent of parental income, social class, etc., except insofar as they affect that ability. Equality of outcome can also be interpreted in a variety of ways: the one adopted in most empirical work is that of reducing differences in standards between schools.

Finally, promoting a sense of social inclusiveness, and perhaps more generally a feeling of fellow citizenship, can be regarded as an essential function of a nation's education system. The idea that schools serve as a melting pot for society, dissolving the cultural divisions that can otherwise create social fragmentation and conflict, is an old one but is still important—especially in a world where migration of various kinds seems to be on the increase.

However, here again there is room for disagreement, especially over the nature of the community in which the child is to be included. Is the relevant community the local one? Or should inclusiveness be defined regionally, nationally, or even internationally? Indeed, is the relevant community necessarily based on geography? For some groups, including their children in religious or ethnic communities might be more important than educating them to be part of the local town, region or nation. And this in turn raises a further question: who is to decide which is the relevant community—the parent, the child, the teacher or the policy maker?

Implicit in most government policy is the assumption that the relevant community is the national one. Hence we shall assume that a policy is undesirable if it does not promote inclusivity between social groups throughout the country as a whole. More specifically, since socioeconomic status and ethnicity are among the most prominent of the current fault lines in society, we shall consider a policy undesirable if, other things being equal, it contributes to school segregation between the better off and the poor and/or between different ethnic groups.

Finally, it is important to note that not all of these ends may be attainable simultaneously. For instance, it may be that the most efficient way of raising the average performance of a school system in terms of educational outcomes is through concentrating resources on the most able, which would in all likelihood violate equity, however the latter is defined. To take another example, some parents might only be satisfied with a school system that allowed them to send their children to schools segregated on religious or social grounds, a decision that might meet the aim of responsiveness, but that could violate the broader aim of social inclusiveness or a national sense of community. In such cases some kind of trade-off between aims may have to be accepted, with, say, more quality being achieved at the expense of some equity, or the promotion of a greater sense of national community at the price of not meeting some parents' desires for segregation.

So what of the various means for achieving these ends? The theoretical arguments that, under certain conditions, the choice-and-competition model for delivering public services can promote quality, efficiency, responsiveness and equity better than alternative models that rely upon trust, command-and-control or voice were laid out in previous chapters. But briefly they run as follows.

If parents can choose which school they send their child to, and if money follows the choice, then schools that succeed in attracting pupils will also attract resources and thrive, whereas those who do not will fail. Schools, interested in their own survival for knavish reasons, knightly reasons or both, will have a strong incentive to raise the quality of the education they provide, and their responsiveness to parents' expressed needs and wants. Schools will also have an incentive to be efficient and innovative, since in that way they will be able to provide a higher quality of education from limited resources. All this is in contrast to the other, no-choice models of service delivery, where such incentives are either absent, feeble or perverse. Also, purchasing power in the choice-and-competition model is equally distributed, and thus helps to promote equitable outcomes—again in contrast to the other models, which generally offer the middle classes greater opportunities than the less well off to manipulate the system.

This is what the theory says. But does it work out like this in practice? As we saw earlier, various countries have experimented with choice and competition in school education. What has happened there? Were these desirable outcomes achieved? And what about the 'extra' aim of education policy that we drew attention to above: social inclusiveness? Was greater quality and efficiency obtained, but at the expense of greater school exclusivity and segregation?

The Impact of Choice and Competition

The evidence on the impact of the choice-and-competition model in practice mostly concerns the experiences of Sweden, New Zealand, the United States, and England and Wales. Unfortunately, it does not cover all of the ends that we have discussed, but usually concentrates on two: educational quality standards, as measured by exam performance; and segregation, as measured by the proportion of different social groups in each school. The evidence has been usefully reviewed by the Prime Minister's Strategy Unit and the Department for Education and Skills in the United Kingdom, by Simon Burgess and colleagues at the Centre for Market and Public Organisation at the University of Bristol, and by Stephen Gorard and colleagues at the University of Wales (PMSU 2006a; Burgess et al. 2005; Gorard et al. 2003; see also Le Grand 2003, chapter 8). What follows draws heavily on these studies.

Parents in Sweden have had a choice between publicly funded independent schools and existing state schools since 1992. A significant number of new independent schools have opened, often innovative in form, and have proved very popular with parents.

It is hard to assess the impact on standards since there are few national tests, but studies suggest that grades in mathematics have improved faster where there is more competition. To quote from one such evaluation:

> The extent of competition from independent schools measured as the proportion of pupils in the municipality that go to independent schools improves both the score on a nationalized, standardized mathematics test and the grades in public schools. ... [T]he improvement is significant both in statistical and quantitative terms. There is no indication that the expansion of independent school has increased total expenditures on schools. Thus the improved results imply that productivity has increased across schools.
>
> Bergström and Sandstrom (2002)

Although there is some anecdotal evidence indicating that some segregation has occurred, there is no hard evidence on the impact of choice on segregation (Swedish National Agency of Education 2003). It is worth noting, however, that a decade after the reforms, Sweden remains overall one of the least segregated countries in the OECD.[1]

New Zealand introduced school choice by parents in 1989. Zoning—allocation of children to schools based on catchment areas—was abolished. Schools were removed from the control of local government and given some budgetary freedoms and freedom to control their own admissions.

Somewhat surprisingly, given that the New Zealand experiment has been the subject of a number of evaluations, there is no evidence as to what happened to standards (Fiske and Ladd 2000; Lauder and Hughes 1999;

---

[1]Programme for International Student Assessment (PISA) 2000 (see www.oecd.org/pisa).

Waslander and Thrupp 1995). But segregation by ethnic group, and to a lesser extent by socio-economic status, allegedly increased. This was attributed by the researchers concerned to a variety of factors, prominent among which were the limited support for transport costs and schools' cream-skimming (that is, selecting pupils who were easier or less costly to teach) through their control over admissions. Government control over admissions was reintroduced in 1999.

However, it should be noted that the near-universal acceptance of the claim that the New Zealand reforms led to increased segregation has been challenged by Gorard et al. (2003, pp. 201–2). They point out that the published results of the project actually show that there was decreased segregation, despite the authors concerned making the opposite interpretation.

The US experience varies by state. Under Florida's A+ programme, children who fail a state-wide standard test are offered a voucher that can be spent at private schools. An evaluation of the programme found that the greater was the degree of threat of losing pupils with vouchers that a school faced, the greater was its improvement in performance (Greene and Winters 2004).

Also in the United States, the Milwaukee Parental Choice Program (MPCP) was introduced in 1989. Parents whose total household income did not exceed 175% of the poverty level were eligible to apply for vouchers for their children to attend secular private schools. The numbers allowed to participate in the programme were capped at 1% of total enrolment in the Milwaukee Public Schools District (MPSD). The voucher was worth $2,500: only 38% of per-pupil funding of students in the MPSD. The MPSD did not lose any money if a child took up a voucher. In

1998, the ceiling on enrolment was lifted to 15%, the value of the voucher was raised to $5,000, 45% of pupil funding began to come from the MPSD, and caps on the proportion of students at participating schools that could be voucher students were lifted.

The official study of the programme only looked at the pre-1998 version (Witte 1997). It compared the performance of voucher students with a randomly selected sample of public-school students and to a random sample of applicants to the scheme who were rejected. Comparison of voucher students with similar public-school students revealed that there were no differences in performance between the two groups and a very weak (and statistically insignificant) advantage in reading scores.

Caroline Hoxby analysed the impact of the post-1998 version of the programme, when incentives were much sharper. She found that, as the degree of competition faced by schools increased, test results improved. Hoxby has also reviewed the evidence on the impact on the performance of public schools of competition from 'choice' schools not only in Milwaukee, but also in Michigan and Arizona. She found evidence of strongly improved performance by the public schools, from which she concluded that the efficiency-inducing effects of competition were more than enough to offset any potential effects of cream-skimming. She also examined the effects of competition with private schools on public schools, and of competition between public schools themselves. Again she found that competition had a positive impact on performance (Hoxby 1994, 2002, 2003).[2]

---

[2]For a critique of some of Hoxby's work, see Rothstein (2005)—and for a (convincing) rebuttal of Rothstein, see Hoxby (2005).

A study of a choice scheme in Chicago found no increase in standards that could be attributed to the programme, but found that there was an increase in segregation by ability. However, under the Chicago scheme, money did not follow the choice and schools could not expand or contract significantly (Cullen et al. 2000).

Parental choice of school has in theory been available for state schools in England and Wales since 1989. Schools have had some freedoms over their budget, and 75% of their budget comes from a per-pupil funding formula, such that the money follows the choice (at least until 2006, when the 75% requirement was dropped). However, because in practice many schools were, and are, oversubscribed, other ways of allocating pupils to schools have been used, including allocation by catchment area and, in some cases, by schools' own admissions rules. In addition, there have been many other changes in education policy since 1989, including the imposition of a national curriculum, the development of national tests together with league tables showing comparative performance of schools in those tests, and, as we saw earlier, various command-and-control measures such as the introduction of a compulsory numeracy and literacy hour. Hence it is difficult to attribute what actually happened to any particular policy development, including those associated with increasing choice and competition.

Nonetheless, there are studies that control for these other factors and hence can produce some evidence concerning the impact of choice and competition. Stephen Bradley and colleagues at the University of Lancaster have demonstrated that areas in the United Kingdom where there is more competition, as measured by school proximity, do appear to perform at a higher level (Bradley and Taylor 2002; Bradley et al. 2001).

Ros Levačić (2004) of the Open University also examined the relationship between competition and performance. She found that competition, as measured in terms of five or more perceived competitors, had a positive and statistically significant impact on examination results. At the national General Certificate of Secondary Education (GCSE) level, the key indicator is five or more high-grade passes (grades A*, A, B and C). Levačić found no impact in terms of the pupils obtaining five or more GCSE passes at grades A* to G, but a positive impact in terms of the proportion of pupils obtaining five or more GCSE passes at grades A* to C. She concluded:

> Schools do respond to competitive pressures to improve a particularly well publicized and widely used performance indicator. This supports the view that competitive pressures do stimulate managers and teachers in schools to improve a measure of performance accorded a high public profile. This only serves to emphasize the importance for the policy of choosing the right indicators in the first place.
>
> Levačić (2004, p. 188)

In apparent contrast, Stephen Gibbons, Stephen Machin and Olmo Silva of the London School of Economics have examined the link between choice, competition and performance of children at primary school in the southeast of England and concluded that, although church schools responded positively to competition, secular schools did not (Gibbons et al. 2006). I say 'apparent' because their initial analyses, using specially devised measures of choice and competition based on actual pupil travel patterns, did find a positive effect of both choice and competition on performance even among secular schools. As they themselves say, 'these estimates suggest small but significant gains to pupils in schools facing more competitive markets' (Gibbons et al. 2006, p. 29). However, although they have devoted some time to constructing their choice-and-competition measures, the researchers argue that drawing conclusions from the simple correlation between them and pupil performance is potentially misleading since the travel patterns on which they are based may themselves have been affected by school performance, rather than the other way round. So they replace them with other measures based on distances from the Local Education Authority boundary, since they argue that the potential for both choice and competition increase as pupils and schools move away from those boundaries; and it is these measures that only show a significant effect with church schools. Which result is accepted will depend on whether one prefers measures of choice and competition based on actual behaviour, with their accompanying problem of possible reverse causation, or those based on 'proxy' measures based on (one kind of) distance, but taking no account of whether the distances concerned actually affect behaviour.

Research by Simon Burgess and colleagues at the University of Bristol indicates that where there is more choice, segregation between schools is higher than segregation between the corresponding neighbourhoods (Burgess et al. 2007). Another study by Burgess shows that when poor and affluent children live in the same general area and have the same measured abilities, the poor child is less likely to go to a good school. However, this is due to the fact that the better off actually live closer to the good schools within the area, and hence are within the relevant catchment zone. If real choice were available, this would reduce the influence of simply living near good schools, and hence could go some way towards rectifying this imbalance (Burgess and Briggs 2006).

On balance, the evidence indicates that, in most of the international cases examined, extending parental choice had a positive impact on standards, not only in the schools that were chosen, but also in the schools that were not. All this suggests that the incentive effects of competition and choice on quality, at least as measured by exam performance, worked as predicted. But there did appear to be negative effects on segregation in some cases, and thus on social inclusiveness, especially if schools were allowed to control their own admissions. This effect was more pronounced where there was little supply-side flexibility.

The next question would therefore seem to be whether it is possible to use this experience, coupled with theoretical insights from the now fairly substantial body of theory on choice and competition, to design a choice system that enhances the positive effects on standards, that improves efficiency and responsiveness, that contributes to greater equality in outcomes, and that reduces segregation—at least when compared with the alternatives. Put another way, what are the conditions that a model based on choice and competition needs to fulfil to meet the aims of education policy?

There are at least three such conditions. They involve increasing the ability of users to make choices; decreasing the ability of providers to make choices; and widening the extent of competition. More specifically, the competition must be real; users must be properly informed, especially ones who are less well off; and opportunities and incentives for selection or cream-skimming must be eliminated.[3]

Competition: Must Be Real

It is in one sense a truism that for the choice-and-competition model to work, the competition must be genuine. But, for that condition to be fulfilled, certain other conditions have to be met. These are that the money must follow the choice; that alternative providers must be available; and that there must be appropriate mechanisms in place to allow new providers to enter the market and failing ones to exit.

Money Must Follow the Choice

Most schools in most countries do intend to, and will certainly claim to, provide a good service. But choice provides a powerful reality check on how far they are succeeding in doing so as far as customers are concerned. The fact that some schools are chosen whereas others are not is acting as a clear signal of success or failure: a signal that is not available in no-choice or monopoly systems, which

[3]In some of the original work on quasi-markets, Will Bartlett and I specified two further conditions for quasi-markets to work well: low transaction costs and providers being at least partly financially motivated (Le Grand and Bartlett, 1993, chapter 2). Most transaction costs in educational quasi-markets involve measures for accounting for the real costs of services that would probably have been introduced under any model of public service delivery if they did not exist already. Motivation issues are discussed in earlier chapters (see also Le Grand (2003), especially the epilogue).

in consequence often find it difficult to distinguish effectively between good and bad performers.

However, the purpose of introducing choice and competition is not simply to provide a signal of success or
failure. All the incentive arguments in favour of choice
are contingent on there being consequences for schools
of being chosen or not. More specifically, there need to be
benefits to schools that are chosen and costs to schools that
are not. Now, whether a school loses or gains pupils affects
professional pride, and that may be sufficient incentive for
the service to generate an improvement in performance.
However, it is unlikely to be sufficient in all, or even in
most, cases. A more powerful way of ensuring that there
are consequences of choice is for funding to follow the
choice: for the schools not chosen to lose resources and
those that are chosen to gain resources.

If funding is to follow the choice, then the money must
be sufficient to create real competition. In the first stage
of the Milwaukee experiment with school vouchers, the
voucher was only worth around a third of the average cost
of education in the state school system. It was not until the
money was increased that behaviour altered significantly.

A further condition is that all the key decision makers
have to be motivated to respond in the desired direction.
For instance, teachers need to be faced with the adverse
consequences of teaching in schools that are not chosen
in order to provide incentives to change their behaviour
in the class room. In Milwaukee again, this was not true
either for schools or for teachers. Individual school funding was not based on the number of pupils, and as a
result there was very little pressure on schools to improve.
Indeed, the initial version of the voucher scheme imposed

no costs on schools losing pupils, thus actually relieving pressure on them rather than the reverse.

If the money is to follow the choice and if that is to have a real effect on school behaviour, then schools need to have independence and control over their budgets. In New Zealand, schools had a separate grant for teachers' salaries and so were limited in their ability to use different kinds of teachers or teachers' assistants. They also had to pay according to national pay rates. In consequence, schools in advantaged areas were better able to attract teachers than those in poorer ones, which in turn contributed to their ability to cream-skim.

In this connection, the current British government proposals for creating 'trust schools' with greater freedoms over their staffing and budgets are very welcome. This follows similar previous initiatives, such as that of the Academies programme, which replaced failing schools with new institutions—again with substantially greater freedoms.

Availability of Alternatives

For school choice to work there must be schools from which to choose. It is often claimed that this condition is rarely fulfilled, even in urban areas. But such claims must be treated cautiously. Take secondary schools in England. Data obtained from the Department for Education and Science show that 32% of maintained mainstream secondary schools in England have two or more schools within one mile of them, 70% within two miles, and 80% within three miles. Since the National Travel Survey shows that the average length of the journey to school for 11–16 year olds in England is three miles, this implies that four-fifths of English schools have at least two other potential choices, attendance at which would entail little if any extra travelling.

If having one other school or more in proximity is regarded as sufficient for choice, then the figures are even more impressive, with 61% of secondary schools having one school or more within one mile, 82% within two miles and 88% within three miles. In short, barely one in ten schools in England has no potential alternative within three miles.

That said, even three miles is a long way to walk (though not to cycle), and help with transport and with transport costs should be available, especially for the less well off. The Sutton Trust and others have published proposals for a comprehensive national school bus network, similar to that prevalent in many parts of North America (Sutton Trust 2005). And the current British government is extending the right to free school transport to children from poorer families to their three nearest secondary schools within a six-mile radius. All of these are moves in the right direction.

Entrance

An important conclusion drawn by Burgess and colleagues from their review of the international evidence was that choice with what they termed supply-side flexibility (that is, the ability to start new schools or close old ones) reduced segregation, while supply-side rigidity increased it (Burgess et al. 2005, p. 19). Supply-side flexibility includes the possibility for popular schools to expand if they wish to, and for new schools to be set up with relative ease. But in many cases neither of these are easy. In

England, committees representing existing state schools (School Organising Committees) have power jointly with the local education authority over the number of school places in an area. They could, and did, use this power to restrict schools expanding and to prevent new schools from entering the market. Such organizations are a classic example of providers clubbing together to protect their interests; they have no place in a properly functioning choice-and-competition model education system. Fortunately, they are to be abolished under current government proposals.

A second issue involves capital funding. If the money following the child is simply sufficient to cover operating costs (as in most systems of choice), then how can new entrants find the capital resources to start up?

In Sweden and the Netherlands, no capital funding is provided by the state; and this can cause problems. In Sweden, for example, 40% of applications to start new independent schools in 2001 that were approved by the National Agency of Education did not result in the school starting due to problems in obtaining facilities and meeting start-up costs (Raham 2002).

However, in the Swedish case at least there are alternative sources of funding. Many of the new independent schools are provided by for-profit corporations who have access to private capital markets. In consequence, despite the lack of state funding, the number of independent schools in Sweden has dramatically increased since the 1992 reforms. Having such alternative sources of finance seems to be an essential condition for new entrants.

In this connection, the current British government proposals for encouraging new entrants do not seem sufficiently ambitious. They encourage private sponsorship of new schools, but do not as yet allow entry by for-profit firms. This seems an unnecessary restriction (it has not been applied, for instance, in social democratic Sweden), and one that could limit some of the gains from increased competition.

However, there cannot be complete freedom of entry. Conditions need to be imposed on new entrants so as to ensure that they provide an education in line with government policy, not only with respect to standards but also with respect to inclusiveness.

Again, Sweden provides an example of the kind of conditions that can be used. The National Agency of Education makes a judgement on whether or not to approve a new school based on the following criteria (PMSU 2006a, p. 10).

(1) The applicants must show that they have the ability to run a school that provides an education that is equal to the education that children would receive at a public school. They must also show that there is a possibility of finding a suitable site for the school and that they have the start-up finances for running the school.

(2) The main content of the curriculum has to be the same as the national curriculum and syllabus. The school will have to provide an education that emphasizes the 'common goals and the fundamental values' of the national curriculum. If the independent school has a religious character, the content of its teaching must not be biased or indoctrinating in any way.

(3) The applicants must show they have enough pupils interested in the school that they wish to operate (a minimum of twenty pupils for a compulsory school).

(4) The school must have teaching staff who have the same qualifications as their counterparts in state schools.

Exit

As well as provisions for dealing with new entrants, it is important to have some means of dealing with school failure: the turning round of failing schools, or allowing them to 'exit'. An important issue concerning exit is that, if the money is following the choice, this could jeopardize the viability of a school without providing an alternative to its remaining users. However, choice can provide effective bottom-up pressure for revealing poor quality and under-performance. Its impact on a school over time can trigger intervention to turn round the service, or to manage its closure, before reaching the point where users might be put at risk.

As in all areas of the economy, there is a danger of destructive political intervention: bailing out failing schools and blunting the incentives within the system. So any intervention should be rules-driven and carried out by an independent agency. This could be a locally elected organization such as the Pupil Advocate, as suggested by the think-tank Policy Exchange (O'Shaughnessy and Leslie 2005), or it could be a national organization similar to the education inspection agency in England, Ofsted, or the Audit Commission. What is key is that, whatever agency is chosen, it is independent of both central and local government.

Choice: Must Be Informed

If parents are to make successful choices of school for their children, they must be properly informed about the quality of the alternatives. There are a variety of ways of giving them the ability to do this.

Swedish examples are again useful here. An annual prospectus of all schools in the City of Stockholm is published by the municipal council, giving a comprehensive profile of all schools in the area, and including some performance-data indicators such as the results in ninth-grade tests and results in city-wide tests at lower grade levels. The prospectus also includes the results of parental-satisfaction surveys carried out on the parents of each school in Stockholm. Naska municipality in Sweden publishes a catalogue that is distributed to parents annually along with their school voucher. The catalogue features a profile on each school, performance data (absolute) for each school, application procedures, dates of open evenings and the results of parental-satisfaction surveys of parents currently at the school.

However, Sweden also provides an example of a potential problem with the information condition: that of potential inequity. A Swedish report revealed that the propensity to make an active choice of school was higher amongst those with greater amounts of education. Around 50% of parents stated that they do not believe they have sufficient information to make an informed choice of school, with those with greater amounts of education more likely to state a belief that they are well informed (PMSU 2006a).

This suggests that a system for parental choice that was concerned with equity would have some means of offering extra support in providing information and other forms of help to the less well off. In this connection, the current British government proposals for establishing dedicated choice advisers to help less well-off parents is of particular interest (Department of Education and Skills 2005). These advisers could be an important tool in promoting both equity, and, through increasing the range of informed choice, the incentive effects of choice and competition on both quality and efficiency.

But there is a further problem with respect to informed choice. What if parents use different criteria to choose schools? Suppose that some parents, instead of concerning themselves with, say, the school's educational standards, are more interested in whether the child is likely to be happy or not, or with the social status of his or her peers, and choose according to those factors. Suppose further that, as popular belief has it, middle class parents are concerned with standards and social status, while working class parents are only concerned with their child's happiness. Would this not create significant problems for the choice-in-education model, both in terms of its ability to promote equity and in terms of the incentives it provides to schools?

Now in one sense, especially if the aim of education policy is parent empowerment, there is no such thing as the wrong criterion. What parents are concerned about is what matters; if they are concerned only about whether their child is happy at school and choose on that basis, then schools will simply compete to make their pupils happy and everyone will be content.

However, this ignores a number of factors. First, as noted before, there are other aims of education policy, and some of the things that parents want may be incompatible with those. Thus parents seeking schools with high social status are almost by definition working against social inclusiveness and equity. Social status is a positional good and cannot be distributed equally.

But here again we have to set the choice policy against other models. In a world where children are allocated to state schools by catchment areas and where there is a parallel system of private schools, parents seeking social status will do so either by moving house or by sending their children to private school. This is a problem for educational policy generally (and indeed for wider society) and can afflict all models, not just the choice-and-competition one.

What criteria do parents actually use for making their choices? There seems to be remarkably little evidence on this. Such as there is, however, suggests that, despite much popular belief to the contrary, working class families seem to have similar educational aspirations for their children as middle class ones. One study by Anne West and colleagues at the London School of Economics found that, regardless of social class, almost all parents wanted their child to stay on at school beyond the age of 16; that, while 87% of middle class families wanted their children to go on to higher education, 83% of working class families wanted their child to do so as well; and that all parents had universally high employment aspirations for their children—again regardless of social class (Noden et al. 1998).

However, the same study also found that, despite their similar aspirations, middle class children tended to end up at higher-performing schools than working class children. This the researchers attributed in part to middle class parents using more tactically effective strategies in making their choices, for instance, more frequently choosing selective schools or taking risks in the ordering of their choices. But the researchers concluded that other factors affecting the actual outcomes were more mundane than this: transport costs and cream-skimming. Middle class children had the resources to travel further if that was necessary to go to a high-performing school; and they were more likely to be accepted for admission once they got there.

What follows from this in terms of policy? Again it suggests that there should be substantial help with transport costs, especially for the less well off; and that there should be restrictions on schools' ability to cream-skim. To this we now turn.

Cream-Skimming: Must Be Avoided

Where schools are oversubscribed and in consequence are able to select their pupils, schools, not parents, will be able to do the choosing. Parental choice will become school choice. The consequence may be segregation or polarization by ability or social group, with popular schools choosing more able children or those from better-off families. Both social inclusiveness and equity would be compromised.

It is not clear how much of this kind of cream-skimming goes on in the United Kingdom. What is clear is that schools that control their own admissions are far more likely to select on the basis of 'cream-skimming' criteria than those who do not. Another study by Anne West and colleagues at the London School of Economics found that 9% of autonomous schools (that is, schools that control their own admissions) selected according to ability compared with just 0.3% of non-autonomous ones. Also, only 15% of autonomous schools included having children with special educational needs as a criterion for a child's admission versus 48% of non-autonomous schools. They also found a range of what they termed 'idiosyncratic' criteria and practices that were potentially unfair, including refusing to admit pupils on the basis of a poor performance at interview, the bad behaviour of siblings already at the school, and, in the case of a Catholic school, whether the parents had also applied to non-Catholic schools (West et al. 2004).

Did these selection processes lead to actual cream-skimming with knock-on consequences for educational performance and segregation? A later study by West and colleagues found that secondary schools in London that controlled their own admissions admitted higher-performing children as measured by the results in the national tests taken at the age of 11, prior to admission to secondary school, than schools where the local authority controlled admissions. In addition, schools with selective/potentially selective criteria admitted even-higher-performing pupils. The percentage of pupils known to be eligible for free school meals was lower in schools that controlled their own admissions as was the percentage of students with special educational needs (West and Hind, forthcoming).

In relation to voluntary-aided schools, other researchers have found that the proportion of pupils known to be eligible for free school meals was lower in both primary and secondary schools compared with the proportion in the local communities (Chamberlain et al. 2006). As West and colleagues point out, it is well established that in general these kinds of school have better exam results. However, we cannot assume straight cause and effect here, since other factors, such as quality of teaching (likely also to be higher in these schools), obviously also affect exam results. The picture seems clearer with segregation: Stephen Gorard found that the ability of schools to control their own admissions was the key factor resulting in increased segregation in their local areas (Gorard et al. 2003).

Faith schools are often singled out as offering high standards of education and obtaining good exam results in consequence. But here again it seems to be selection that is playing the key role. LSE researchers Gibbons and Silva (2006) have found that faith primary schools had a very small impact on pupils' progress:

> There is clear positive selection into Faith schools (and into schools that have autonomous admissions and governance arrangements) on the basis of observable characteristics that are favourable to education—even when we compare pupils that originate in the same block of residential housing.

They suggest that 'any performance impact from "Faith" schools in England seems to be linked to autonomous governance and admissions arrangements, and not to religious affiliation' (Gibbons and Silva 2006, pp. 28, 29).

The problem is also found in New Zealand, where polarization or segregation apparently emerged as a problem following the introduction of school choice. There, oversubscribed schools were able to introduce 'enrolment criteria', the content of which was lightly regulated, with schools only having a legal requirement to abide by the Human Rights Act and the Race Relations Act (with few controls against covertly operating outside these laws).

So, in the event of a school having more applicants than it had places, schools could choose which children attended the school. Popular schools were able to expand. However, funding for this was limited, and, in any case, many schools were reluctant to expand as they wished to maintain their exclusivity and their ability to pick their students.

A further incentive to cream-skim arises if parents can top up funding, formally or informally. Again the New Zealand example is instructive. Most schools expect parents to pay 'voluntary fees' to contribute towards the cost of running a school. Locally generated revenue is significant as a source of school revenue at secondary level (for urban schools). Obviously, parents who have less income can less afford these 'voluntary contributions', so schools with an intake of children from predominantly poor backgrounds receive significantly less funding from this source than those with children from better-off families. While it is illegal to discriminate against children whose parents do not wish to/cannot pay this voluntary contribution, when schools can choose their students it is likely to be a consideration in a principal's decision about whether or not to admit a student if they are poor.

In contrast, in Sweden each independent school must agree to a maximum number of pupil admissions with the National Agency of Education. If applications to the school in any year exceed this number, enrolment criteria involving either waiting lists (first come, first served) or a random lottery must be established. Most independent schools use enrolment criteria based on waiting lists. Although this is superior to most other methods of selection it does contain its own biases: it is likely to favour the more highly educated groups in society (as they are likely to be better informed). Also, for the most-desired schools in Sweden this has resulted in all students at the schools having birthdays in the first half of the year (as children are placed on school waiting lists as soon as they are born). However, there is another example in Sweden of the dangers of selection. The City of Stockholm municipality introduced selection by ability in upper secondary schools in 2000. This resulted in an increase in segregation by ability (unsurprisingly), but also by immigration and socio-economic status (Söderström and Uusitalo 2005).

Another factor which may encourage schools to discriminate (where possible) against lower socio-economic groups in enrolment criteria is the benefits-in-kind possible through unpaid work at the school from enrolling children whose parents are professionals (versus, for example, children whose parents are in manual work and are low skilled). The decentralization of administrative functions to the local level that inevitably accompanies the choice-and-competition model probably leads to these benefits-in-kind becoming more important to schools, and a lack of qualified parent volunteers may lead to disadvantaged schools spending more to obtain these specialist services than advantaged schools do.

The Swedish example suggests that it is possible to design choice systems that do not encourage cream-skimming. In fact, there are at least three basic ways in which this might be done in the education context.

One is to restrict, or even completely remove, the ability of the school to make its own admissions decisions. Schools could be compelled to take pupils from a range of backgrounds by a banding or quota system. Alternatively, popular schools could be compelled to have a waiting list from which potential entrants were chosen by lottery (as is now being tried by several English local authorities).

Removing or restricting schools' power over admissions and compelling them to take certain kinds of pupil is essentially a command-and-control policy and has the advantages of all such policies: it is clear, relatively simple and easy to implement. On the other hand, it also has that model's disadvantages. It offers nothing by way of positive motivation to the school to take on more difficult pupils; indeed, it is more likely to breed resentment, perhaps directed at the children themselves, among the staff concerned. Even more problematic, it does not offer any incentive to keep the children in school or do anything positive with them once they have actually been admitted—unless it is accompanied by other command-and-control measures such as restrictions on schools' powers of exclusion.

A second possibility is to have completely free entry, refusing to permit schools to turn pupils away.[4] So, if a school has a good reputation and so virtually all parents want to send their children there, the school will become overcrowded. Indeed it might become, in the short term, massively overcrowded. So be it. The extra resources might buy in extra teachers to keep the pupil–teacher ratio down but there will be overcrowded classrooms, tuition in the corridors perhaps, and the quality of staff may be driven down as teachers have to be hired at the last moment when it is realized how many children have chosen to go there in the current year. The poor school will now have fewer pupils, and in the short term at least lower teacher–pupil ratios, and it will have lots of

[4] I am grateful to Geoffrey Brennan for suggesting this possibility.

space, and so may become attractive to parents. An equilibrium could be achieved that might satisfy the requirements of both choice and equity. Where children go to school will be completely driven by choice. And equity would be satisfied because of choice—some parents preferring the quality staff of the good school, and some preferring the absence of crowding in the poor school.

However, many will find this completely laissez-faire approach unattractive, not least because of the short-term effects on the good school and its existing pupils. Instead of relying upon this, or upon the command-and-control option of restricting schools' powers over admissions, a third option would be to use the power positive incentives to encourage schools to take on children from poorer families. Such children could attract a 'disadvantage premium': an extra amount per child from a disadvantaged background. This requires more attention than is possible here, and so is discussed in detail in chapter 5.

Conclusion

Choice-and-competition systems can achieve the ends of educational policy. But they must be properly designed so as to meet the conditions for effectiveness. There must be mechanisms for ensuring that the entrance for new providers is easy, that exit can take place and that the relevant decisions are immune from political interference; that parents are given the relevant information and help in making choices, especially parents who are less well off; that there is help with transport costs, preferably again targeted at the less well off. And the opportunities and incentives for cream-skimming should be eliminated.

CHAPTER FOUR
Health Care

Both the current British government and the principal opposition party are committed to increasing patient
choice in the provision of publicly funded health care.
Other countries are also moving in this direction, including Norway, Sweden, Denmark and the Netherlands.
Many continental European countries, especially those,
such as Germany and France, whose health systems have a
tradition of being financed through social insurance, have
long offered patients choices of various kinds, including
choice of providers. And in the United States, patients
have historically had considerable freedom to choose their
clinician or hospital, even within the publicly funded systems of Medicare (for the elderly) and Medicaid (for the
poor).

However, the policy is controversial. In Germany and
France, some of its perceived disadvantages have led to
moves to restrict patient choice of provider. In the United
States there has been a growth of so-called 'preferred-
provider' organizations, with insurers trying to direct
patient choices towards particular providers (with whom
they have negotiated discounts). In the United Kingdom,
where the idea of empowering patients in any form is a

relatively recent innovation, patient choice remains highly contested territory.

The debate has many dimensions. The policy's advocates claim that, coupled with competition, extending patient choice will improve both the quality of health care and the efficiency and responsiveness with which it is delivered. And, through providing the less well off with a counterpoint to the power of middle class 'voice', it will make the system more equitable. Its critics argue that patients are too ill informed or just too ill to make sensible choices, that opening up the system to competition will simply create opportunities for unscrupulous providers to exploit people's vulnerability by over-treating them, and that the whole process will involve an unacceptable level of administrative costs.

Previous chapters have argued that, in general, the choice-and-competition model for delivering public services is indeed an effective instrument for improving the quality, efficiency, responsiveness and equity of those services—especially when compared with the alternatives. However, the critics of the model have a point (indeed several points), for the model will only achieve these desirable ends under the right conditions. As with the similar arguments in the context of education, the design of the relevant policy instruments so that these conditions are fulfilled is crucial.[1]

This chapter deals, therefore, with some specific issues concerning the appropriate policy design that arise in applying the choice-and-competition model in the context of health care. It starts with a brief review of the general

[1]Other useful discussions of the issues raised in this chapter include Stevens (2004) and Farrington-Douglas and Allen (2005).

arguments of the previous chapters concerning the ends and means of public services, and applies them to health care. It then reviews such empirical evidence as exists concerning the impact of choice and competition in various countries that have implemented the model in the provision of health care. Finally, it draws on that evidence and on other work to specify some of the conditions for the successful implementation of that model. In each case it tries to specify how policy may be designed to ensure that, so far as possible, those conditions are met. There is a brief conclusion.

Ends and Means

The ends for public services were discussed in general terms in chapters 1 and 2. They included quality, efficiency, responsiveness and equity. The previous chapter illustrated how they could be applied in education; many of the same arguments apply in health care. The principal problems of interpretation arise in the case of quality and equity. Quality could refer to the quality of inputs, processes, outputs and outcomes. Inputs in this case refer to the quality of professionals and of the medical facilities; processes to waiting times and the courtesy and consideration with which patients are treated; outputs to the treatments themselves; and outcomes to improvements in health that result from treatment. Unlike in education, where most of the debate concerns outputs or outcomes (usually measured by performance in national tests), the debate in health care often focuses heavily on process issues, such as waiting times—especially in countries such as the United Kingdom where this aspect of quality has historically been a major problem.

Equity can be defined in a variety of ways in the health care context, including equality of access, equal treatment for equal need and equality of outcomes. In practice, the extent of inequity is usually measured by differences between social groups in their utilization of health care services relative to their need—that is, the extent to which equal treatment for equal need is achieved—and this is the interpretation we follow here.

What of means? The previous chapters have laid out in some detail the general arguments as to why using the choice-and-competition model to deliver public services to achieve these ends is likely to be generally more effective than the no-choice models involving trust, command-and-control and voice. Applied to the provision of health care, they run as follows.

In a no-choice world of publicly funded health care, patients who are dissatisfied with the quality of the treatment they are getting, or the responsiveness of the medical professionals or managers with whom they are dealing, have only a limited range of options open to them. If there is a private health care sector running in parallel to the public one, they can use that—or, at least, the wealthier among them can do so. Those who cannot afford this option can only complain, either directly to the professional or manager concerned or to their superiors. In each case, the individual has to depend for a response on the goodwill, or knightliness, of the person to whom they are complaining. As well as being demanding to undertake, this is a fragile mechanism for improving quality. It offers little or no direct incentives for improvement to the knavish, self-interested professional or manager; and even knightly, more altruistic ones do not always respond well to being challenged by pushy patients.

Moreover, insofar as complaining works at all, it favours the self-confident and articulate middle classes, thus tending to steer services in their direction at the expense of the less well off. The middle classes thus have a double advantage over the less well off. They are better placed to persuade the public service to meet their needs; and, if their powers of persuasion prove inadequate to get them the service they want, they can turn to the private sector.

In contrast, in a world where choice and competition is the norm, patients dissatisfied with the quality of service they are getting from a provider of medical services—a hospital or a GP practice—have the opportunity to go to another who can provide them with a better service. If the money follows the choice, then the hospital or practice that provides the better service will gain resources; that which provides the inferior service will lose. Whether the unsatisfactory provider is a knight or a knave, they will wish to continue in business; the knave because it is in his or her self-interest to do so, the knight because he or she wants to continue to provide a good service to needy patients. But, in order to continue in business, they will have to improve the quality and responsiveness of the service they provide, as well as the efficiency with which it is delivered. Moreover, equity is promoted by the fact that the less well off can now exit if necessary, and that they are no longer dependent on their ability to persuade professionals to give them the service they want.

Of course, there are limitations to the applicability of these kinds of argument to all forms of health care. Patients who have suffered an accident or are seriously ill are unlikely to be able to make any kind of choice of provider, and may have to rely upon others (attending doctors or ambulance crews) to make the choice for them. Some forms of medical treatment are one-offs (your appendix can only be taken out once); in such cases, information gained about the quality of treatment may be of little use in deciding where to go for other forms of treatment. Some people—perhaps an elderly person or one suffering from a debilitating long-term condition—may prefer not to have to make the necessary decisions: 'doctor, you decide'.

However, the number of conditions where choice is impossible or unwanted should not be exaggerated. The number of so-called 'blue-light' attendances at hospital accident and emergency departments where patients are actually unconscious or seriously ill is relatively small.[2] Experience of one form of treatment at a hospital can give insights into the quality of care provided for other treatments at the same facility. And, as we saw in chapter 2, the recent British Social Attitudes Survey showed that most people do want choice of medical facility—with, interestingly, larger majorities in favour of choice among the less well off than among the middle classes.

So much for the theory. But do things really work that way in practice? Can the model really deliver in the way described? Or is it actually beset by too many practical difficulties to operate effectively in the real world? What has been the experience of the various countries that have been experimenting with the choice-and-competition model?

The Impact of Choice and Competition

As we discussed above, forms of patient choice and hospital competition exist in a number of countries throughout

[2]It can be as low as 1% of all attendances (5% of ambulance attendances): figures taken from www.chrisgrayling.net / hospital / 20040520_workingpaper6.htm, accessed 7 January 2007.

the world, including Norway, Sweden, Denmark, the Netherlands, France, Germany and the United States. However, for most of these countries there has been relatively little research into their impact. The principal exception is the United States—perhaps not surprisingly since the American health care market is, at least in form, probably the most competitive health care market in the world.

However, we must be careful not to make too simplistic a comparison between the US health system and those of other countries, since it has several features that are not replicated elsewhere. These include, notoriously, a lack of universal coverage, a phenomenon that in large part derives from its other unusual features, such as a heavy reliance upon employer-based finance and on private insurance. Further, the usefulness of US evidence is complicated by the fact that the structure of the US market has changed over time. In the 1980s users were covered by generous insurance and hospitals were fully reimbursed for their costs. This led to what some authors have described as a medical arms race, where hospitals competed with each other on inputs: the quality and quantity of physicians and of medical facilities. In the 1990s, the Medicare system introduced fixed 'prospective payments'—that is, a fixed price for every course of treatment—and utilization reviews, whereby doctors had to justify to the payers that the treatment they were providing was suitable; and private insurers followed suit. This was accompanied by the growth of Health Maintenance Organizations (HMOs), in which prospective patients enrol, paying a fixed annual fee and receiving all the treatment they need without paying further.

Despite all this, there are some generalizations that can be made from the US experience. Carol Propper and colleagues from the University of Bristol's Centre for Market and Public Organization have recently produced a comprehensive survey of the US and other international evidence concerning the effects of competition between providers, especially hospitals.[3] They found evidence that competition in the United States with fixed prices both reduced costs and increased quality (usually defined in terms of health outputs, such as the number of deaths after emergency admissions for heart attacks), especially in markets where HMO penetration was high. There were other more specific findings, including one that the effect of competition was to give more appropriate treatment, with sick patients in less competitive markets receiving less intensive treatment with worse health outcomes than they did in more competitive ones.

There is also evidence from the United States that, when patients deliberately choose not to go to their local medical facility for treatment but choose to go further afield, their health outcomes are better. For instance, Lamont et al. (2003, p. 1375) concluded from a study of cancer patients in Chicago that

> patients who were able and willing to (1) research therapeutic outcomes and (2) find and expand the resources necessary to then receive these therapies seem to fare better than those patients who end up at the closest place for care, even if their diseases and treatments are apparently the same. Moreover, the difference was quite substantial, with a distance of ten miles being associated with as much of a decrease

[3]See Burgess et al. (2005) and also Propper et al. (2006). Also, Gaynor (2006) provides a useful review of the US evidence and Fotaki et al. (2006) that for the United Kingdom.

in risk as a pack–year of cigarette smoking [an extra pack of twenty cigarettes a day for a year] was associated with an increase in risk.

One interpretation of this is that exercising choice is good for one's health: that the sense of control that choice gives has a powerful effect on individuals' ability to respond to treatment and their speed of recovery.

But the United States also provides useful examples of where problems can arise.[4] Statistical information provided to patients on quality was often too complex to be used effectively by them or indeed by institutional buyers of health care. In fact, it was most widely used by the providers of that care itself, sometimes in ways that may have harmed patients. In an echo of our discussion of targets in chapter 1, providers concentrated on improving what was measured, which was not necessarily that which contributed to health. The fixed-price system may have induced 'cream-skimming', whereby hospitals tried to attract patients whose treatment costs they expected to be below the fixed price they were being offered, and to 'dump' patients whose costs they expected to be above that price. In areas where prices were not fixed, hospitals appeared to cut both prices and quality, relying upon the fact that the users and purchasers of health care find it difficult properly to assess quality and hence to observe quality reduction (Gaynor 2006).

There are also useful lessons to be derived from the British experience with the NHS 'internal market' that was

[4]For a useful critique of the principal features of the US system, but one whose conclusions differ in some respects from those reported here, see the works of the Harvard Business School economist Michael Porter, the most recent of which is Porter and Teisberg (2006).

introduced by the Conservative government in 1991, and which lasted until the Conservatives lost the election of 1997. The principal feature of that market (and one that remains under the current system, at least in England) was a splitting up of the old state monolithic bureaucracy into 'purchasers' and 'providers'. The providers, mostly hospitals, became semi-independent 'trusts', with freedom to price their services and to compete for custom from the purchasers. The purchasers were of two kinds. There were GP 'fundholders': family practices who not only provided primary care for the patients registered with the practice but also held a budget to purchase some forms of secondary care (mostly elective surgery) for them. And there were health authorities: geographically defined organizations who purchased all secondary-care services for those who lived in their area, except for those purchased by fundholders.

Under the auspices of the Kings Fund, Nicholas Mays, Jo Mulligan and I undertook a comprehensive review of the evidence concerning the effectiveness of the internal market with respect to quality, efficiency, responsiveness, accountability and equity (Le Grand et al. 1998). Combining the outcomes of this with the results of some later work yields the following conclusions.

During the period from 1991 to 1997, NHS activity rose faster than resources (and rose at a relatively faster rate than before the reforms). This suggests that overall, despite some well-publicized increases in transaction costs, there was an increase in efficiency in the NHS that was attributable to those reforms. Moreover, following the partial roll-back of the internal market that was introduced by the new government in 1997, efficiency fell (Le Grand 2002).

Although many analysts predicted that cream-skimming would cause equity problems, no cream-skimming was observed in practice. The principal equity concern arose from the differences between the two types of purchaser, one of which, GP fundholders, was more successful in getting a better deal for their patients. In particular, GP fundholders were effective in bringing down waiting times, reducing hospital referrals and holding down prescription costs. They were also better able to generate surpluses on their budgets than health authorities, and were able to generate improvements in the responsiveness of providers.

There was no evidence of any increase in choice for patients, and although there were changes over the period in indicators of quality such as waiting lists and patient satisfaction surveys, it was difficult to attribute these to the reforms. One study, however, found an increase in mortality from heart attacks in hospitals that were under greater competitive pressure (Propper et al. 2004). This may have been the result of the fact that, unlike the US examples cited above and the current UK quasi-market, prices were not fixed. In that situation, economic theory would predict that competition can lead to price and quality cutting—unlike the situation where prices are fixed. Here, theory would predict that competition will lead to improvements in quality. Since that is now the only dimension on which competitors can compete.

Overall, despite some changes in culture, measurable changes were relatively small, and perhaps not as great as was predicted by the reforms' advocates, or as was feared by their critics. This appears to have been because competition within the market was limited, and this in turn may have been because some of the essential conditions

for the market to operate were not fulfilled. More specifically, the incentives for the market players were too weak
and the constraints imposed by central government were
too strong. This interpretation is reinforced by the fact that
the area where there were the greatest changes, GP fund-
holding, was the one where the incentives were greatest
and the constraints the weakest.

Finally, there is evidence from the choice experiments
tried out in England, the popularity of which was referred
to in previous chapters (Coulter et al. 2005; Dawson et al.
2004). It will be recalled that these offered a choice of
hospital to patients who had been waiting more than six
months. Help with transport costs was provided, and
each patient was given an adviser to help him or her
with the relevant choices—points to which we shall return
below.

Take-up of choice was high—perhaps not surprisingly
given that the patients concerned had already been waiting six months. Significantly, there was no difference in
take-up between different socio-economic groups, with
one exception: the unemployed took up the offer of choice
less frequently than the employed. The pilots also had a
significant impact on waiting times in the areas in which
they operated.

So what are the lessons that can be learned from all
this about policy design? It will not surprise the atten-
tive reader that these conditions are the same as those
for applying the choice-and-competition model in education—at least in broad outline. The principal ones may
be summarized under the headings of competition (it
must be real), choice (it must be informed) and cream-
skimming (it must be avoided).

Competition: Must Be Real

As we have seen in earlier chapters, for the choice-and-competition model to work—that is, for it to provide the incentives for greater quality, efficiency and responsiveness—there have to be competitors, actual and/or potential. That is, there have to be alternative providers from which to choose; there have to be easy ways for new providers to enter the market, and, correspondingly, for failing providers to leave or exit from it; and there have to be ways of preventing existing providers engaging in anti-competitive behaviour, such as colluding with one another against the interests of users, or trying to create local (or even national) monopolies. In short, the competition must be real.

Availability of Alternatives

For choice to exist, and for competition to be real, there must be alternative providers from whom to choose. It is often argued that this condition is not fulfilled in many public services: in particular, that offering choice is illusory, especially in health care and education. In Britain, London is usually cited as an exception; but most of the population outside of London cannot realistically be offered a choice of schools or hospitals simply because there are not enough of them within easy travelling distance—or so the argument goes.

However, the facts do not bear out this claim, at least for English hospitals (for the facts on schools, see the previous chapter). A study by the Kings Fund and the University of Bristol found that 92% of the population had two or more acute NHS trusts within sixty minutes travelling time by car. Further, 98% of the population had access to 100 or more available and *unoccupied* NHS beds and 76% to 500 (Damiani et al. 2005). The only areas that came close to monopolistic provision were the relatively lightly populated parts of Cornwall, North Devon, Lincolnshire and Cumbria. (In passing, it might be noted that these figures also suggest that, at least at the time of the study, 2001, there was considerable underutilized capacity in the English NHS. This was in a period of lengthy waiting lists, and does not reflect well on the combination of trust and command-and-control models of service delivery that were in use at that time.[5])

What the argument that choice is illusory ignores, but that is evidenced by these figures, is just how urbanized the British population is. Almost 90% of the population lives in urban areas, with over half the population resident in just sixty-six conurbations with populations of 100,000 or more (Denham and White 1998). There are problems of potential monopoly in rural areas; but the numbers of people affected are relatively few, and their situation should not be used to prevent the implementation of a policy in the rest of the country if there are good reasons to implement it there. The rural tail should not wag the urban dog.

And in fact there are ways of introducing competitive pressures even in places where there are geographical monopolies. These could include 'franchising': where a local monopoly service is offered to a single provider under a contract after a competitive bidding process. The contract is for a given period so, at the end of the

[5]See Stevens (2004) and Le Grand (2002) for discussion of the evolution of British policy towards the NHS under the early years of the Labour government.

period (of, say, five years), the bidding process would be repeated. Instead of competition *within* the market, there would be competition *for* the market. There are problems with franchising—how to encourage long-term investment when the investor is only guaranteed a contract for five years, how to avoid the incumbent having an advantage when the bidding process is repeated—but these are not insuperable.

All that said, there is evidence that some patients, notably those from poorer backgrounds, do have problems with transport to medical facilities. A survey of the evidence undertaken by myself and colleagues at the Department of Health and the LSE suggested that, perhaps rather surprisingly, the poor did not necessarily have to travel further in terms of distance than the better off to access good medical facilities in the United Kingdom at present. However, even if the actual distances were not a factor in deterring the poor from using the NHS, the *cost* of travelling those distances, or, more generally, access to transport, was important. More specifically, lower car ownership and the consequent dependence on public transport among lower-income groups was a significant factor in lower utilization rates and higher rates of failing to attend appointments (Dixon et al. 2003)[6].

So, both to promote equity and to help make competition real, an essential element of any policy aimed at encouraging choice is the provision of help with transport and travel costs. This might involve the better planning of public transport infrastructures and timetables to enable easier access to a range of health facilities at all times,

[6]A shorter version of this reference is Dixon et al. (forthcoming).

or transportation arrangements being made on behalf of patients by the NHS. Ideally, financial help would cover the full range of costs, including the costs of time off work and costs associated with having an accompanying partner or carer.[7]

Although this may sound potentially quite expensive in terms of public expenditure, in fact it might not involve a great deal of extra cost to the public purse, at least in England. We saw above that the distance to travel to obtain a range of medical facilities is not vast for the urbanized parts of the United Kingdom. And in fact there is already a hospital travel-costs scheme, targeted on patients assessed as low income or who have to travel frequently over long distances.[8] It includes patients needing transfer for elective treatment and chronic care and non-emergency release from accident and emergency. According to data from 1999/2000[9] there were 12.5 million patient journeys for non-emergency travel for which claims with a total cost of £150 million were made (or £12 per journey on average). Even if, under the more ambitious scheme proposed here, these costs were to more than triple, they would not involve enormous sums—especially when set against an overall budget for the English NHS of £70 billion.

Entrance

One of the interesting findings of research into the factors that lead to improvements in productivity in areas

[7]For more specific suggestions in the context of the British NHS, see Farrington-Douglas and Allen (2005).

[8]These groups are currently entitled to free (non-emergency) transport for themselves and, where considered medically necessary, their escorts.

[9]Department of Health, personal communication.

outside of health care concerns the importance of encouraging new types of provider to enter the market. Jonathan Haskel and colleagues examined the productivity of all UK manufacturing plants between 1980 and 1992 and found an interesting pattern over time. There was a growth in productivity during that period; but at least half of this was the result of the entry of new, high-productivity providers and the exit of old, low-productivity ones. The rest of the growth arose from competitive pressure on existing firms and from changes in the ownership structure in those firms. It seemed as though new blood was essential to generate efficiencies and to increase productivity (Disney et al. 2003).

Of course these findings relate to manufacturing industry, not to health care, but there does not seem to be any reason why something similar should not apply there too. In this connection, it is of interest to observe some of the early effects of the new specialized treatment centres that the UK Department of Health has contracted from the independent sector to provide services for NHS patients. Although it is difficult to make direct comparisons (largely because of data deficiencies within the NHS itself), such data as there are suggest that these independent treatment centres are significantly more productive, with shorter lengths of stay and more innovative practices, than their equivalents within the NHS (Department of Health 2006).

To avoid possible problems developing with quality and efficiency, new providers should be vetted before they are allowed to enter the market. Care needs to be taken with this, though, to ensure that this vetting procedure is not 'captured' by existing providers and used as a barrier to keep out potential competitors. The vetting should therefore be undertaken by an agency that is independent of existing providers and, since government would undoubtedly be subject to lobbying by these providers, independent of government as well.

New providers face other barriers to entry into a market. An obvious one in health care is the capital cost of setting up a new facility; this could be quite considerable, especially if high technology equipment is required. A less obvious one concerns the habits of users. If people are used to being referred to their local hospital (and if GPs are used to referring them there), then it can be difficult to persuade them to use a new or a different provider. In such cases it may be necessary to offer some kind of assistance to new providers, for instance, through guaranteeing them a higher price for their services, or by guaranteeing a specific volume of business. However, such assistance should be strictly time limited.[10]

Exit

Then there is the crucial question of 'exit', or, more generally, how to deal with failing hospitals or other medical facilities. It is critical for the choice-and-competition model that there is some mechanism for dealing with failure that imposes costs on failing institutions. For, if there is no cost to failure, then many of the incentives that are so important for generating the desired outcomes disappear.

[10]The early rounds of independent-sector treatment centres mentioned above had both kinds of assistance: a price that was on average 11% higher than the standard NHS price and a guaranteed contract. However, neither of these forms of assistance were on offer for the later rounds.

We saw in a previous chapter the problems that this absence of penalties for failure (indeed, its apparent rewarding) has generated for the Welsh NHS as it tried to use the trust model of delivery. Arguably, the development of a similar phenomenon was one of the reasons why the internal market of the 1990s NHS failed to generate large changes in behaviour. Relatively early on in the market's lifetime, a major teaching hospital in London got into trouble because it was losing business to outer-London hospitals. There was considerable political protest, a consequence of which was that the hospital concerned was bailed out and the internal market in London suspended. As a result, not only was the incentive for that hospital to improve removed, but, even more seriously, it had the effect of serving notice on hospitals, managers and consultants round the country that financial failure not only would not be penalized, but may even be rewarded—with a consequent dramatic weakening of incentives throughout the system.

Now, dealing with inefficient or ineffective providers presents perennial difficulties for all systems of public service delivery, including models based on voice, trust and command-and-control, as well as those based on choice. Failure has considerable costs in every system, not least for the people who work in the facility concerned. But those other models have an additional difficulty. Quality failure is obscured because, in the absence of choice, people still have to keep going to the facility concerned, however unhappy they might be with the service they are receiving; there is no obvious drop-off in demand (although there may be an increase in complaints, if the relevant voice mechanisms are working properly). And financial failure is often concealed, partly because accounting procedures tend to be less rigorous in these models than under choice and competition, but more because in these situations money is often simply handed over by the budgetary authorities to bail out providers in financial difficulty (a phenomenon in turn facilitated by the lax accounting procedures).

In contrast, failure under choice and competition is obvious. If a hospital or other medical facility is failing in terms of quality, and if it is recognized to be doing so by potential users, then it will not be chosen. In consequence its revenues will fall, and its quality failure will be reflected in financial failure. The failure will be clear; moreover, it will affect relatively few people directly. Hence it will not be necessary to have some additional mechanism for checking quality; and, if it becomes necessary to close the facility, there will be relatively few patients affected.

However, the very clarity of the failure process in the choice-and-competition model creates, or rather exacerbates, a further problem. This is the danger of political interventions to prevent that failure. Such interventions are very hard for ministers and other politicians to resist in any public system for which they are perceived to be responsible. In 2001, a British member of parliament from the ruling Labour party lost his seat at Kidderminster to a doctor, Richard Taylor, who stood against him to defend a local hospital threatened with downgrading by a command-and-control decision of the local health authority.

But these kinds of intervention are particularly serious in the case of choice-and-competition models, as the experience of the London internal market indicates. For, by protecting hospitals and other medical facilities from the consequences of losing patients, they blunt the incentives to improve, not only for the hospital itself but, via osmosis, throughout the system.

How can destructive political intervention be avoided? Part of the answer is to have procedures for dealing with failure that are rule driven, and that allow little opportunity for discretion and hence for political intervention. One such rule could be that intervention would be triggered automatically if, as Keith Palmer, an expert on failure regimes, has suggested, a provider has deficits exceeding 3% of total income for two consecutive years (Palmer 2005, p. 21).[11]

But possibly even more important than the existence of rules governing the process of intervention is a requirement that both the decision to intervene and the intervention itself are undertaken by an agency independent of government. This could be an industry regulator: as in the privatized utilities in the United Kingdom, where regulators have statutory powers to act to protect consumers in the event that the utility should face financial distress or fail. In those cases the regulator does not have to wait until a firm becomes insolvent to act and its powers enable it to approve or reject a financial restructuring (Palmer 2005, p. 17).

In fact, in one part of the NHS an agency exists that already has similar powers. This is Monitor, a regulator with responsibility for Foundation Trusts. Foundation Trusts are mainly hospital providers within the British NHS, publicly funded and owned, but operating

---

[11] For a useful comparative study of regulation in different countries, see Lewis et al. (2006).

independently of the Department of Health. Monitor has
the responsibility of assessing their eligibility to become
a Foundation Trust in the first place and then of ensuring that they continue to meet the conditions for eligibility, especially with respect to financial health and
the type of and quality of the service that they are
offering.

A useful illustration of how an independent agency can
work to insulate government from political fallout is the
experience of Monitor and the Bradford Teaching Hospitals NHS Foundation Trust. Fairly soon after it had become
a Foundation Trust, the Bradford hospital realized that it
was heading for a substantial deficit, initially estimated
at around 6% of its turnover, but possibly much larger.
Monitor became aware of the problem a few months later
through its routine monitoring procedures. It called in
consultants, who wrote a report that was highly critical
of the Trust's management and of its systems, especially
its financial ones. The trust was deeply unhappy with the
consultants' report, but Monitor accepted its conclusions
and used its intervention powers to appoint a new chairman, who then reshaped the board by bringing in a new
chief executive and finance director. A financial recovery
plan was produced proposing efficient savings through
a variety of measures, including procurement improvements, increased theatre utilization and a reduced length
of inpatient stay, and with about a 6% reduction in staff.
The plan was successful, with a turnaround in the Trust's
performance and the virtual elimination of the deficit
within twelve months.

The key feature of the Bradford story was that there
was no political intervention. This was despite pressures
to intervene on ministers (and on 10 Downing Street) from

local MPs. But ministers (and Number 10) were able to stand back because action was being taken by Monitor. In consequence, a successful turnaround was achieved without a bail-out and incentives were preserved.

Anti-Competitive Behaviour

There is a danger in any market that the actors in the market will behave in ways that damage competition. Examples include agreements to drive up prices, arrangements to divide up the market and not to poach on each other's territory, and attempts to try to take over competitors so as to create a monopoly.

It might be thought that such knavish behaviour would not be a characteristic of the health care quasi-market. In most such markets, many of the key providers are non-profit, voluntary or public organizations, and it might be expected that they would behave in a less self-interested fashion: that is, more like knights than knaves. As the University of Bristol study cited above notes, this view has actually permeated several court judgements about anti-competitive behaviour in the US health care market. One court judgement stated that 'The Board of the University Hospital is simply above collusion' (Burgess et al. 2005, p. 27).

However, as the Bristol study goes on to point out, the evidence on the behaviour of non-profit organizations in the United States does not support this view. These organizations use market power in the same way as for-profit ones, with, for instance, hospital mergers leading to price increases. Even the knightly activity of providing care to those who cannot pay (so-called 'uncompensated care') does not differ in extent between for-profits and non-profits.[12]

So it is likely that, even in health care quasi-markets with a high proportion of non-profit or public organizations, there will be a need for a policy to deal with anti-competitive behaviour. Again to prevent unwarranted or unhelpful political interference, the answer here would seem to be to have a rule-driven system implemented by an independent regulator. It would in fact be sensible for this regulator to be the same as that for deciding upon the entry and exit of providers; for all the relevant decisions are aspects of competition and indeed all are part of the business of making competition real.

Choice: Must Be Informed

In previous chapters we have emphasized the importance of information if the choice-and-competition model is to work. More specifically, for choice to act as an effective driver of quality, it is necessary to rely upon the user's judgement about the quality and responsiveness of the service and for providers to react to choices made on the basis of those judgements.

In health care this is clearly a key issue, since much of the relevant information is of a technical nature that most patients will have difficulty dealing with. And in fact there is little evidence that, when presented with information about, for instance, the quality of outcomes by individual surgeons, patients actually use that information to make

[12] The non-profit/for-profit terminology, although widely used, is slightly misleading. Both types of organization make profits (or try to); non-profits, however, do not distribute profit to shareholders or other types of owner, but re-invest it in the operation.

the appropriate judgements (Burgess et al. 2005, p. 3; Hibbard 2003; Marshall et al. 2000).

However, all is not lost. Even if not driven by patient choice, there is evidence that providers do use published information to improve their performance—even if, as noted earlier, in doing so they sometimes engage in some dubious manoeuvres to massage the figures. This may be because of professional pride (the naming and shaming phenomenon discussed in a previous chapter), or because they believe that, although patients do not directly use the information, it will eventually affect patient choice through the impact on their reputation.

Moreover, there are ways of making information more accessible and more usable by patients. Some of these have been usefully summarized by Judith Hibbard of the University of Oregon (Hibbard and Peters 2003).[13] They include processes for lowering the effort required via computer-aided decision tools and visual symbols (such as star ratings of medical facilities); helping people to have a better idea of what the actual experience resulting from a certain choice might be like (through narratives or stories); and highlighting the meaning of the information by 'framing' it appropriately. As an example of the last, people find it easier to understand frequencies ('2 in every 100 people get complications from this procedure') than probabilities ('there is a 2% probability of complications from this procedure').

One innovation that proved very successful in helping overcome the patient-information problem and encouraging user choice in the United Kingdom was the Patient

[13]See also Farrington-Douglas and Allen (2005) for a useful discussion of how the information needs of particular disadvantaged groups could be met.

Care Adviser (PCA) in the choice pilots mentioned above. PCAs were trained staff, sometimes with a clinical background, who advised on choice of provider; they also gave advice on other matters, including (from those who were clinically trained) clinical ones, and offered support and reassurance.

This idea could be extended. The responsibilities of this role could include monitoring care plans, offering choices of provider, discussing treatment options, identifying special needs regarding travel, disability (mobility) and language (communication), providing information and updates about the care pathway (including assessment, treatment and aftercare), booking appointments with providers, arranging transport, helping patients navigate the system, and supporting/coaching patients on self-care, self-management and behavioural change. Another advantage of this scheme is that, depending on who the PCA is, the scheme could draw on existing skills: nurses, pharmacists (for medical regimes), or even ex-patients (for mental health, for instance).

One potential criticism of the PCA idea is that it could be resource intensive. This would be especially likely if a new professional role was created, generating an 'army of bureaucrats'. On the other hand, this would be less likely if the scheme drew upon existing skills. And there could be resource savings. It could lead to better use of hospital capacity, more informed and active patients taking responsibility for their health and care, lower rates of non-attendance, and better coordination and planning of care. It could release GPs' and consultants' time. Further, the cost could be reduced if the scheme were targeted at poor areas—those where the biggest equity problems are likely to arise.

Care would have to be taken that the PCA did not become another layer of professionals between the patient and the service, and also that the scheme did not encourage increased patient dependence. In this connection, it is worth noting that there are other positions in most health services that fulfil some of the proposed PCA functions already, such as cancer or diabetic nurse specialists, and patient advocates. In other areas of public services, such as employment services, advisors have been introduced—again very successfully. A priority therefore would be to establish what is already happening both within the health service and in other areas, to learn from the relevant experience and to build on it.

Cream-Skimming: Must Be Avoided[14]

In health systems with consumer choice of multiple insurers, cream-skimming can arise on the insurance side, where insurers try to select good health risks as enrollees and discourage worse health risks or charge them higher premiums. In social insurance systems with multiple funds, where funds can choose whom they accept as members, they try to select below-average-risk enrollees. In systems such as the one in the United Kingdom where purchasers have a defined population, the problem is confined to the provider side, whereby GP practices or hospitals may try to select patients who are easier or cheaper to deal with. The consequence is discrimination against groups with a higher risk of ill health, such as the old and the poor.

[14]This section and the other parts of this chapter are based on Dixon and Le Grand (2006). I am grateful to Anna Dixon for allowing me to use the material here.

Here we are primarily concerned with the application of the choice-and-competition model to the choice-of-provider model. And it will help focus the discussion if we concentrate on a particular case: that of the British NHS.

Both the incentives to cream-skim and the opportunities for doing so are undoubtedly present in the NHS. As GPs currently receive the majority of their resources on the basis of capitation, there is a strong incentive for them to cream-skim low-risk patients who will consume fewer resources. The opportunity presents itself in a number of ways, including refusing to sign patients on or taking patients off the list. There is no hard evidence of which we are aware that this occurs in practice, though there is much anecdote.

The situation with respect to hospitals is a little more complicated. The lower the health risk associated with patients admitted for hospital treatment, the less resources they require, the greater their chances of a speedier recovery and the quicker they can be discharged. Thus giving preference to lower-risk patients helps both the finances of a hospital and its ability to meet government targets such as reducing waiting lists.

This incentive is now being increased by the current adoption throughout the NHS of a fixed-price system: so-called 'payment-by-results', which fixes the price or 'tariff' for each procedure. As we saw earlier in the US case, fixed prices do offer an incentive to cream-skim, whereby hospitals try to attract patients whose treatment costs they expect to be below the fixed price they are being offered and to 'dump' patients whose costs they expect to be above that price.

There are thus significant incentives to cream-skim. The fact that most hospitals have long waiting lists that include both high- and low-risk patients gives extensive opportunities for those incentives to be exercised. But there are also factors that militate against both hospital and GP cream-skimming. There is first the question of knowledge: can those in charge of acceptance on a GP list or in charge of hospital outpatient referral effectively distinguish between high- and low-risk patients? Second, there are professional ethics, or 'knightly' motivations. Doctors do not like turning away needy patients; indeed the duties of a doctor as set out by the General Medical Council include to 'make the care of your patient your first concern' and 'make sure that your personal beliefs do not prejudice your patients' care' (General Medical Council 2006). Third, there are professional interests: more difficult patients may present more of an intellectual challenge (although, of course, for doctors in search of a quiet life this could act as a positive incentive for cream-skimming).

It is worth noting that, in hospitals at least, these incentives not to cream-skim are largely associated with consultants, whereas the direct incentives to cream-skim (finance, the pressure to reduce waiting lists) impact primarily on hospital management. Much research indicates that it is consultants who are the principal decision makers in NHS hospitals (Crilly and Le Grand 2004), suggesting that perhaps the incentives not to cream-skim may currently dominate the incentives to do so.

The situation is complicated further by the increasing use by NHS purchasers of private providers, such as treatment centres and mental health services. For it could be argued that the incentives to cream-skim are intensified in a profit-making context: that private providers are run by 'knaves' not knights, and hence will ruthlessly exploit any opportunity they have to enhance their profits, including the opportunities offered by cream-skimming. This is clearly a danger, although again it is likely to be partly offset by the fact that some of the 'private' organizations concerned are in fact non-profits, and hence are likely to have a more complicated (and more knightly) motivational structure than that of simple maximization of profit.

We have seen that incentives and opportunities for risk selection or cream-skimming exist in the current NHS, although we have been unable to find direct evidence of its prevalence. Will the introduction of patient choice for elective surgery and other forms of non-emergency treatment make things better or worse?

If patient choice is coupled with payment-by-results using a fixed-price or tariff system, in the absence of any corrective action, the answer is that it will probably make things worse, at least from the perspective of incentives. With a fixed tariff, hospitals have a strong incentive to take patients whose treatment will cost less than the tariff, and an equally strong incentive not to take patients whose treatment will cost more. Moreover, the fact that the payment for each patient will be so transparent, and that the rewards for cream-skimming will therefore be so clear, is likely to accentuate the effect. Again this may be partly or wholly offset by professional ethics and interests, and the power of professionals to control admissions.

With respect to opportunities, the position will depend on the effects of patient choice on waiting lists. A hospital without waiting lists can still cream-skim if those in charge of admissions judge that a particular patient will cost more than the tariff they will receive and have the right to refuse treatment. But then the hospital is likely to be operating significantly under capacity. Such overt refusal to treat patients when capacity exists is likely to be noticed by GPs, who would identify hospitals that were 'dumping' patients and could then use their purchasing decisions to challenge this. So if the extension of choice and expansion of capacity leads to an elimination of waiting lists or even a substantial shortening overall, this could reduce the opportunities for cream-skimming. On the other hand, if some popular hospitals acquire a longer waiting list as a consequence of patient choice, then their cream-skimming opportunities at least are increased.

Hospitals could also cream-skim in less overt ways. For instance, a hospital could locate in a more affluent area where on average the local population will be lower risk. A hospital could decide not to have an accident and emergency department, thereby excluding all emergency (and more expensive) admissions, an access route that is also more prevalent among lower socio-economic groups. The hospital could market its services at targeted populations of lower risk, and perhaps at more affluent patients. Or it could alter the case mix of its patients by providing only limited intensive care facilities (although this would only systematically discriminate against lower socio-economic groups to the extent that they have more co-morbidities).

Overall, it seems likely that there will be some negative impact on equity arising from patient choice enhancing cream-skimming effects. So what to do?

One possibility is to introduce some kind of stop-loss insurance scheme whereby hospitals faced with a patient whose treatment costs lie well outside the normal range get allocated extra resources once the cost has passed a certain threshold. These would have to be justified as catastrophic costs (not as the result of poor-quality care). This has the advantage of removing the incentive to discriminate against high-cost patients, but carries with it the problem that the hospitals concerned have no incentive to economize on treatment once the threshold has been passed.

A similar scheme was used to stop cream-skimming by GP fundholders (which had been signalled as a potentially significant problem for the scheme at the time of its introduction (Scheffler 1989)). There it seemed to have worked, with little or no cream-skimming being observed during the duration of the scheme (Goodwin 1998).

A second possibility is to take the admission decisions away from hospitals completely. The PCTs or GP practices would 'own' the waiting or referrals list, and hospitals and other treatment centres would be required to accept whoever was referred to them by GPs or PCTs. In fact, this is already envisaged with the introduction of e-booking and choice at the point of referral.

A third alternative is to risk-adjust the tariff system such that higher-risk patients have a higher tariff associated with them. A certain amount of this is already going to happen under the payment-by-results national tariff system. If fully risk adjusted, this could eliminate the incentive to cream-skim completely. However, as has often been demonstrated, risk adjustment is a complex and difficult business; perfectly accurate risk adjustment is arguably an impossible task. But so long as risk adjustment is not perfect, there will remain an incentive to cream-skim. Risk-adjusted payments also provide an incentive to up-code patients to more lucrative high-cost categories.

A form of risk adjustment that would be rather simpler and would help assuage any socio-economic inequities arising from cream-skimming would be to deprivation-adjust the tariff. The tariff could be associated inversely with an area deprivation index such that treatments for patients from deprived areas would carry a higher tariff than treatments for those from wealthier ones. This could in fact be a form of risk adjustment since it is widely believed that, other things being equal, poor people do recover from various forms of treatment more slowly than their better-off peers.

Overall, we do not know whether risk selection or cream-skimming will turn out to be a problem associated with extending patient choice. As the policy is implemented, an equity audit needs to be undertaken, partly to check on the progress of the supported choice package, but also to assess whether there are adverse equity consequences arising from risk selection. If this does emerge as a concern, policy options for dealing with it need to be explored.

Conclusion

Choice-and-competition systems can achieve the ends of health care policy. But they must be properly designed so as to meet the conditions for effectiveness. There must be mechanisms for ensuring that the entrance for new providers is easy; that exit can take place and that the relevant decisions are immune from political interference; that patients are given the relevant information and help in making choices, especially patients that are less well off; and that there is help with transport costs, preferably again targeted at the less well off. Also, the opportunities and incentives for cream-skimming should be eliminated, either through not allowing providers to determine their own admissions or through properly risk adjusting the fixed-price system.

CHAPTER FIVE
New Ideas

So far in this book we have concentrated mostly on examining choice and competition policies that have either already been implemented or are in the process of being implemented. This chapter is more speculative. It looks at some of the possible ways to go beyond these policies and to extend some of the basic ideas into other areas. However, rather than a general treatment that would mean going over ground that has already been covered, it seems better to provide some concrete illustrations of the ways in which this extension might be done. So the chapter concentrates on three specific ideas, each of which develops one aspect of the earlier discussions. One concerns extending the choice-of-provider idea in health care to another aspect of choice, that of treatment, through the development of patient budgets. Another develops a proposal, the disadvantage premium, for harnessing the power of positive incentives to improve the education of the less well off. Finally, the third puts forward the idea of a new kind of provider, the social care practice, that could offer choice in an area of public services where in Britain at least it is very limited: that of the social care of looked-after children.

Patient Budgets

So far we have confined our discussion in health care to
choice of provider. Here we discuss a more extended form
of choice: giving patients budgets from which they can
choose their treatment and the provider of that treatment.[1]
A similar idea, called 'direct payments', has already been
pioneered for social care for disabled people in the United
Kingdom and elsewhere, so we provide a brief description
of the ways in which it has been applied (see also Glasby
and Littlechild 2002). We then consider some of the ways
in which the idea could be applied in health care, and
appraise some of its merits and demerits.

Direct Payments in Social Care

So-called 'direct payments' in the United Kingdom are
cash payments made by local authorities directly to disabled people and other groups to enable them to purchase the services they have been assessed as needing.[2]
Originally, the scheme was confined to service users aged
between eighteen and sixty-five, but it has been extended
to include older people, younger people between sixteen
and seventeen, carers, and parents of disabled children.
The services concerned include disability aids, personal

[1]For other discussions of this idea see Spiers (2003, chapter 12),
Glasby (forthcoming) and Leece and Bornat (2006).

[2]'Direct payments' is an unsatisfactory term in many ways: it
is not very descriptive of the actual policy (the payments are not
always direct, and in some cases may not even involve payments)
and it can be confused with other government policies (such as
paying old-age pensions through bank accounts instead of through
post offices). However, we stick with it here since it is the term
commonly used to describe the scheme.

assistance, short-term breaks and live-in care. It is an alternative to the traditional system of social-care provision in the United Kingdom, where local authorities have acted as direct providers of these services.

Under present organizational arrangements, a bank account is needed for receiving direct payments. Local authorities make it clear what the money can and cannot be spent on; and the user must record how the money is spent. Some use bookkeepers, or an appropriate agency, to do this; and most authorities have set up direct payment support teams to help. Also, each authority must have in place detailed financial monitoring procedures for audit purposes, to fulfil its obligation to ensure that public funds are spent to produce the intended outcomes.

No national evaluation of the direct payments scheme has yet been undertaken. However, there have been a number of evaluations of individual schemes, all favourable. A review of the operation of the scheme in Scotland came to the following conclusion.

> There is strong evidence that direct payments can increase the choice and control recipients exercise over their own lives. This is particularly dramatic when contrasted with the lack of choice and control recipients experienced in some local authority-provided services. ... It should be stressed that recipients identified very few disadvantages to direct payments.
>
> Witcher et al. (2000, paragraph 7.6)

Recipients themselves are very positive about the scheme. Typical comments from disabled individuals include the following.

Things couldn't be better now. It's given me much more freedom and control and I play a more active role in family life. Choice, freedom and control sums it up for me. It has been amazing, my life has completely changed.

Witcher et al. (2000, paragraph 6.106)

A survey of the literature on direct payments comments:

A significant feature of the findings from the various pieces of research and evaluation has been how the quality of life of the disabled person on the scheme has improved. The sense of feeling in control has been a central aspect in all the findings, which again illustrates the empowering experience of the direct payments schemes.... Choice and flexibility were the other themes, which were constantly expressed through all the reports. The other significant point to mention which was highlighted by the report ... was the cost-effectiveness of the scheme compared with an in-house direct service provision.

Hasler (2003, p. 1)

Older people receiving direct payments reported feeling happier, more motivated and having a better quality of life than they did before. There was a positive impact upon their social, emotional and physical health. Further, direct payments have been used to meet specific individual needs, for example allowing people from minority ethnic groups to employ personal assistants that speak the same language as they do (Joseph Rowntree Foundation 2004).

As noted by Hasler (2003), a further advantage of direct payments schemes is that they seem to generate greater value for money. The experience has demonstrated that directly provided services are more expensive than those purchased through the direct payments scheme, with the latter costing 20–40% less than the equivalent services provided in-house.

Local authorities, care managers and social workers often tend to be resistant to implementing the scheme, citing in explanation excessive paperwork, pressure of time and inability of clients to handle the responsibility. Experience with the schemes in operation, however, generates more positive attitudes among these groups.

The Prime Minister's Strategy Unit (PMSU) has proposed combining different funding streams into 'individual budgets', thus:

> helping disabled people to achieve independent living by moving progressively to individual budgets for disabled people, drawing together the services to which they are entitled and giving them greater choice over the mix of support they receive in the form of cash and/or direct provision of services.
>
> PMSU (2005, p. 7)

All these proposals have been endorsed in a Social Care Green Paper, which argued that

> [a]ll groups have the potential to benefit from the opportunity to have greater control over the services they need, and how these should be provided, in a way that offers the real benefits of choice and control of direct payments without the potential burdens. Therefore ... we propose to test the introduction of

individual budgets for adults with a disability or with an assessed need for social support.

Department of Health (2005c, p. 11)

And indeed, at the time of writing, tests of the feasibility of individual budgets are being undertaken by the Department of Health together with other government departments at thirteen pilot sites throughout the country.

Direct Payments in Health Care

At the moment, direct payments cannot legally be used to purchase health care in the United Kingdom, but many have talked about the possibility of extending the social care scheme to areas of health care. Jennifer Rankin of the Institute for Public Policy Research has suggested that mental health service users be given a form of direct payments that she calls 'personal recovery budgets' (Rankin 2005). Mental health was also picked as a possible area for experimenting with direct payments in a consultation process with users, patient organizations, NHS trusts and Strategic Health Authorities that the UK Department of Health conducted in the run-up to their paper on patient choice (Department of Health 2003). One specific comment was that, 'direct payments is one option to extend choice in mental health'. Other areas were also picked out as possibilities for extending direct payments in the consultation, for instance, 'the direct payments system could be extended to other care and treatment, e.g. vouchers for maternity services'.[3]

---

[3]Both quotations were supplied by the Department of Health from their records of the choice consultation.

The NHS Confederation in its reply to the consultation on choice said, 'there would be significant benefits from using direct payments for a number of conditions in terms of empowering patients', although it then went on to discuss some of the problems with the approach (NHS Confederation 2003, p. 19).

Caroline Glendinning and colleagues from the National Primary Care Research and Development Centre at the University of Manchester interviewed fifteen disabled people in receipt of direct payments in social care (Glendinning et al. 2000). Most reported that they did in fact use the payments to purchase elements of health care, including physiotherapy, the management of incontinence, and chiropody. They also wanted the opportunity to purchase a much wider range of health-related services.

In December 2004, Jon Glasby of the University of Birmingham's Health Service Management Centre ran a small private seminar for key stakeholders to explore the issues in more detail. A paper summarizing the discussions concluded:

> As a first step there was a degree of consensus that there would be immediate scope to extend direct payments to small and relatively discrete areas of health care such as people with complex needs already receiving direct payments for their social care needs. Other areas for early consideration might include continuing health care and long-term care, as well as health equipment and palliative, and terminal care.
>
> Glasby and Hasler (2004, p. 14)

The charity Macmillan Cancer Relief has plans to pilot a system of direct payments for cancer patients to buy the care they prioritize and need. Although initially confined to what we would conventionally consider to be forms of social care (gardening, shopping, personal care, domiciliary care), the scheme may be expanded to enable them to purchase what Macmillan call 'total care': the joining up of all the services people affected by cancer need and want. They are also now considering the provision of an electronic card topped up with 'caremiles' that can be used to purchase services. Users would be supported by a Macmillan personal shopper.

Although, as noted above, the best legal advice is that social care direct payments cannot currently be used in the United Kingdom for health services, and that NHS funds cannot be used to make direct payments, in practice there are cases where this has happened, albeit in a roundabout fashion. One is the high-profile Pointon case (eventually subject to an ombudsman's ruling) where a primary care trust paid for the cost of a respite carer for a patient with Alzheimer's disease, Mr Pointon, through a package of direct payments organized by the local social services department.

Direct Payments in Other Countries

The positive experience of direct payments in social care in the United Kingdom is echoed internationally. The Medicaid Cash and Counseling programme in the United States gives eligible beneficiaries who choose to participate a monthly allowance to purchase disability-related goods and services (including hiring relatives as workers). The programme also provides counselling and fiscal assistance and allows users to designate representatives (such as family members) to make decisions on their behalf. An evaluation of the programme in the US states of Arkansas, Florida and New Jersey found that it decreased users' unmet needs, increased their satisfaction with care and did not increase the likelihood of adverse health events compared with a control group (Foster et al. 2003).

A three-year follow-up to the Arkansas evaluation using treatment and control groups found that the treatment group had higher Medicaid costs than the control group. But this was because many of the controls received no paid help and in all they obtained only two-thirds of the services to which they were entitled. Moreover, by the end of the second year these higher personal-care expenditures were offset by lower spending on nursing homes and other Medicaid services (Dale et al. 2003).

Several Scandinavian countries use direct payments in social care. Municipalities in Sweden and Denmark have systems of cash payments for elderly and physically disabled people to purchase personal care, and to some extent for mentally disabled people to do the same. Again these have proved very popular with recipients and their success has led to proposals to extend the schemes to include aspects of health care (Abildgaard and Vad 2003).

In the United States there have been some attempts actually to extend the idea to health care. There are experiments under way using budgets for patients with mental health difficulties in Michigan and Oregon. The Community Mental Health Service Program in Michigan offers opportunities for adults with developmental difficulties or mental illness to control their specialty mental health services, with individual budget holding as part of this. Oregon's scheme gives individuals with developmental difficulties control over a wide range of services through an individual budget, including occupational and physical therapy, transport, employment, family training, personal and home care. Individual preferences are acted on by a broker rather than by the individual directly making cash purchases.

In 2003 President Bush signed into law a system of Health Savings Accounts (HSAs) that has some similarities with the direct payments scheme. An HSA is an account into which individuals and their employers can make tax-free payments to save for future medical expenses. To qualify, individuals have to also have a high-deductible insurance policy to cover large or unexpected medical bills. Funds remain in the account from year to year: there is no 'use it or lose it' rule. When the individual dies, the spouse becomes the owner of the account and can use it as if it were their own HSA. If the individual is unmarried, or upon the death of the spouse, the account ceases to be specifically an HSA and becomes part of the person's estate to be passed on to beneficiaries like any other asset.

HSAs differ from what we call patient budgets in that the money does not come from government funds (except indirectly via the tax-privileging of the accounts), and they are not tied to a particular diagnosis or assessment of need. However, they play a similar role in giving users a greater degree of control over the care they receive, and incentives to use resources in a fashion that meets users' wants and needs.[4] Now Florida, South Carolina and West Virginia are planning to introduce HSAs as part of the Medicaid programme for helping the less well off; these will involve

---

[4]For a critique of HSAs see Enthoven (2006); for a more positive view see Turner (2005).

government money and will be used to allow Medicaid beneficiaries to purchase health insurance in some cases or direct services in others (Milligan et al. 2006).

How Would Patient Budgets in Health Care Work?

As we have seen, direct payments in social care in the United Kingdom and other countries have improved services, reduced costs and empowered users. We have also seen that many have suggested that the idea of direct payments be extended to health care: that is, to offer what we shall term 'patient budgets'. If such a scheme were to be developed in the United Kingdom and elsewhere, how exactly would it work, and would it yield equivalent benefits?

First, how it would work. A prospective patient would visit a GP with symptoms of ill health or with some other condition that needed care (such as pregnancy). The GP would provide a diagnosis of the patient's condition. Each diagnosis would have a budget associated with it, calculated to be enough to pay for the relevant treatment. Depending on the diagnosis, this could be quite simple: a course of physiotherapy for a muscle strain, for instance. The recommended treatment could be elective surgery, in which case the budget would be the current 'tariff' or price for the procedure concerned. In the case of long-term conditions, the budget might be the cost of a package of predictable care for that condition over a year. In the case of multiple conditions, it would be the sum of the costs of the appropriate packages.

Patients would be offered advice by the GP or other medical professionals as to how to 'spend' their budget. In fact, in many cases the GP would undoubtedly play a considerable role in advising the patient and the decision would effectively be a joint one: what is called shared or co-decision-making in the literature. The only decisions that the patient would have to make is what treatment they wanted and which provider they wanted to provide it, from among all the treatments and providers that fell within the budget constraint. And, if they preferred, they could simply hand the responsibility entirely back to the GP: 'Doctor, you decide'.

In a similar fashion to direct payments in social care, patients could be offered the budget in cash. They would then have to account for it, as the recipients of direct payments in social care do. But, except perhaps in long-term care (to be discussed below), this would be unnecessarily cumbersome. For one-off episodes of ill health, it would be enough simply to offer patients a menu of choices of treatments and providers that fell within the budget constraint. In such cases, the patient need not even know that there was a budget underlying the menu. The menu would only include treatments that had met approved guidelines for cost-effectiveness where they were available; and it would only include providers that were accredited by the appropriate authorities.

What would the benefits from such a proposal be? It would have the advantages of extending patient choice of provider coupled with the money following the choice that were discussed in the previous chapter. Providers would be subject to contestability—not only providers of elective surgery, as under current policies, but providers of all the services where the idea was applied, from physiotherapy to those providing care for long-term conditions. This would give them strong incentives to offer services in a cost-effective fashion that were responsive to the needs and wants of patients. A related advantage is that the introduction of patient budgets in certain areas would increase capacity by creating markets for services such as physiotherapy that are often artificially constrained because they are not social care and have a low priority in health.

But the patient budgets proposal would do more than promote provider responsiveness, efficiency and capacity. All the evidence on direct payments in social care and elsewhere suggests that giving people greater control over their situation improves their morale and contributes to their physical and mental well-being. And patient budgets give patients that greater control.

For patient budgets promote not only choice of provider but also choice of treatment. Take mental health services for mild to moderate depression. At present, patients diagnosed with these conditions are usually offered some form of drug treatment. But surveys tell us that many would prefer not to take drugs but to receive some form of talking therapy, such as cognitive behavioural therapy— treatment that, we might note in passing, has been shown to be at least as cost-effective as drug therapies (Centre for Economic Performance 2006). Under the direct payments system, they would be able to choose which they preferred.

Another example concerns palliative care for the dying. Most people diagnosed with a terminal illness would prefer to die at home. But only one in five actually do. The majority die where they least want to: in a hospital (Taylor 2004). And this uses up scarce hospital resources: in Nine Wells, Dundee, for instance, 70% of oncology beds are filled with patients receiving palliative care (personal communication). Allowing more people to die at home would result in considerable savings for the NHS: a rough estimate suggests that the cost to the NHS of a patient receiving palliative home care is about half that of hospital care (Taylor 2004). As Tom Hughes-Hallet, the chief executive of Marie Curie Cancer Care says: 'It's time to give every person the choice they should have over where they die' (Hughes-Hallet 2005, p. 30).

Yet another example is maternity services. Direct payments would be particularly appropriate in this area. Each mother would be allocated a budget from which she could choose home or hospital birth. In fact it used to be the case that women in the United Kingdom had a legal right to a home-birth service. However, it appears that they no longer do (they have the right to a home birth, but only with NHS support if it is deemed 'clinically appropriate'). In fact, only 2.2% of births in England are at home (in Scotland it is just 1%). There seems to be little hard data on UK women's preferences for home over hospital birth, but most experts seem to agree that demand for home birth would be much greater than 2% if support were readily available. Moreover, home birth costs less than hospital birth. In the United States the average uncomplicated vaginal birth costs 68% less in a home than in a hospital (Anderson and Anderson 1999); in the United Kingdom, the National Birthday Trust (1997) came to a similar conclusion. So again, offering choice here through a direct payments route would both empower patients and lower costs.

Long-term conditions present an even more interesting opportunity. Patients with long-term health problems have the potential to become expert in managing their condition, at times more so than the relevant professionals. This has been recognized in the UK Department of Health's Expert Patient Programme (EPP), which, through the provision of courses and other educational tools, assists patients in condition management.[5] A preliminary evaluation of the programme suggests it has been rather successful (Department of Health 2005b). Four to six months after attending the EPP course there was a statistically significant decrease in participants' use of some of the most frequently used care services; GP consultations decreased by 7%, outpatient appointments by 10% and A&E attendances by 16%. There was also a decrease in the use of some of the other care services, such as hospital admissions and use of rehabilitation services and complementary therapies, although these changes were not statistically significant. Other results indicated an increase in participants' confidence, an increase in the use of pharmacy services and health information, and participants feeling better prepared in their consultations with health professionals.

How would it work? For each patient a full assessment of predictable long-term care needs would be made, and the resource implications for, say, a year would be costed to determine the budget. This budget would be given to patients in cash as with the social care direct payments; he or she would be able to use it to purchase the care they chose. This might involve organizing their own care; or, if they preferred, it could be handed over to a care-manager (nurse, community matron or GP) to manage for them. Patients (or the care-manager) would have to account for the way in which the cash was spent.

It should be emphasized that the budget would be expected to cover only predictable care, not emergency

[5]For more information concerning this and other current initiatives aimed at increasing patient involvement in, and control over, their own case, see Caton (2006).

care. So if, for instance, a patient with a long-term condition had to go to hospital because of an unexpected development in his or her condition, this would not be counted against the budget he or she held for that condition.

The payment could take the form of a 'credit card' of the kind being considered by Macmillan Cancer Relief (mentioned above), where a fixed amount of money is put on a card that can then be used to make the relevant purchases. This would both be convenient for users and would provide a simple accounting and audit trail.

A further advantage is that, for those who were eligible for both social and long-term health care, the scheme could actually be merged with the social care direct payment scheme. Patients could be assessed for the totality of their needs, and not suffer from the often artificial distinction between social and health care. As well as for long-term conditions, this would be an advantage for other areas where the boundary between health and social care seems particularly arbitrary, such as maternity services.

Direct payments would not only provide incentives for provider improvement, therefore, but would also empower patients through increasing their range of choice of provider and through offering them choice of treatment. But there are a number of objections to the idea that we must now consider.

Objections

One possible difficulty can be dismissed relatively quickly. A conventional argument against offering patients choice of treatment is that they will always choose the most expensive. In fact this turns out not always to be true, especially where invasive surgery is concerned—although it is probably more accurate for drug treatments. But in any case the idea of direct payments—with a menu of choices to be paid out of a fixed budget—provides budgetary safeguards against this danger.

A more powerful objection concerns patient capabilities and attitudes. It could be argued that patients have neither the knowledge nor the expertise to make the 'right' choices. Would they not make unreasonable or irrational demands? Further, even if they have the right knowledge and information, are people who are sick really in a position to make these kinds of decisions? More fundamentally, would they *want* to make these decisions? The onset of illness makes many people feel feeble and vulnerable; would they not prefer to hand over all the relevant decisions to the medical professionals who, after all, know what they are doing?

The most comprehensive review of the literature on patient decision-making found mixed results from studies of patient preferences on this issue, with some suggesting that many patients actively wanted to be involved in the relevant decisions while others (chiefly the older and less educated) preferred not to be. But overall the review's author concluded:

> [W]hen patients are given the opportunity to make informed choices, they usually welcome it. Unreasonable or irrational demands are not as common as many clinicians fear. Patients often prefer more conservative and cheaper treatments than their doctors are inclined to recommend. Shared decision-making could be one of the best ways to ensure more appropriate uses of health care resources.
>
> Coulter (2002, p. 47)

Moreover, as noted above, there would be nothing compulsory about the scheme. If patient preferred to leave the relevant decisions to the doctor, they would be perfectly at liberty to do so.

A related potential difficulty concerns rationing. The budget would make it clear to patients exactly how much was available to be spent on their treatment—and how much was not available. Whether this is a disadvantage of the scheme or actually one of its merits is debatable. It could be argued that making the limits to spending overt will simply encourage patient dissatisfaction and make them more likely to press for services that the system cannot afford to provide. Alternatively, the very transparency of the scheme could be viewed as a desirable feature. For it removes the deception involved in most less overt systems—the deception being that no rationing is going on—and treats patients as responsible citizens who are aware of all the considerations that concern the relative availability of care for themselves and others.

In fact, the evidence concerning patients' views on rationing supports both points of view. For it suggests that patients prefer rationing to be explicit; but this is partly because they are then in a better position to evade it either by paying for extra services themselves or through protest (Coast 2001; Schwappach and Koeck 2004).

What of the attitudes of providers—doctors, nurses and others who work in the health care system? As we saw, direct payments in social care in the United Kingdom have aroused resistance among providers of care, from local authorities to social workers. An evaluation of the expert patient programme revealed relatively little enthusiasm from doctors for the scheme, a reaction that, with tactful phrasing, the researchers partly attributed to 'the desire of primary care professionals to be the centre of care for people with long-term conditions' (Kennedy et al. 2005, Executive Summary, p. 6). If primary care practitioners do indeed have this desire, then they are likely to be even more threatened by patient budgets than by the expert patient programme, since the former transfers yet more power to patients.

I suspect some resistance of this kind will be inevitable—especially among GPs. However, it may not necessarily be universal, or even long-lasting. An increasing number of health care professionals may find the sharing of responsibility with patients that is implicit in the patient budgets idea attractive.

Another potential problem concerns transaction costs, and the availability of the services required. To make sure that the relevant services were available in the 'market', some set-up costs might be required (as, for instance, in the case of cognitive behavioural therapy, where the appropriate therapists have to be trained). But, if patient needs are to be met appropriately, much of this will have to be done anyway. Also, there will have to be a costing of all the relevant services, so that a charge for them can be set against the relevant budget. But any system for the efficient allocation of resources requires the proper costing of treatments; and most health systems are developing mechanisms for doing this in any case.

Last, but not least, is the question of topping-up and equity. If the topping-up of the budget from a patient's own resources were allowed, this would favour the better off and violate the principle of health care being provided only on the basis of need. In fact, the topping-up issue does not really arise in the menu-based approach;

most patients would not know that there was even a budget to be topped up, and the practice could simply not be permitted (as is the situation at present in the United Kingdom with elective surgery). It would be most salient in the case of payment budgets for long-term care, especially if it were merged with direct payments for social care (where topping up is allowed in the United Kingdom). However, if it were thought undesirable in this area, again it could simply not be permitted for health care purchases, with the accounting procedures acting as a monitoring device to ensure that the prohibition was not infringed.

Considerations of equity raise an issue that might well appeal to a different part of the political spectrum. Might it be possible to offer larger budgets to those from poorer backgrounds? This could be justified on straightforward redistributive grounds. Or it could be argued on the grounds of clinical need: that, because of poorer nutrition, housing and environmental conditions, those from poor areas with a given condition needed larger amounts of care to achieve the same improvement in health than those from more privileged backgrounds.

Whether the poor should receive more health care than the better off for the same condition raises issues that are well beyond the question of patient budgets. However, the point is worth noting in this context as an illustration of the more general point that these kinds of ideas for empowering service users could be used to achieve centre-left ends as well as right-wing ones, and that they should not therefore be automatically assigned to any particular part of the political spectrum.

Patient Budgets: The Way to Go?

Patient budgets in health care could both empower patients and give incentives to medical providers to offer better and more responsive health care. They could extend choice of treatment and choice of provider. They could reduce costs and improve services. And, most importantly, they could improve patients' health and well-being. They would not be suitable for all forms of health care, most obviously those for which patients are acutely ill and incapable of making any kind of decision for themselves. But for other conditions, so long as they were predictable and/or long term, patient budgets may be a useful way forward.

The Disadvantage Premium

In our discussion of education in chapter 3 we noted that cream-skimming—the deliberate selection of children by schools so as to improve the school's performance in league tables or other indicators of quality—was a significant problem for the choice-and-competition model in that area. We discussed ways of dealing with it, including not allowing schools to control their own admissions or compelling them to accept everyone who applied. However, each of these methods involved restricting schools' freedom of action in some way with the demoralizing effects that such restrictions always bring and the dangers of encouraging evasion.

Rather than restriction, it might be better to employ the power of positive incentives to combat cream-skimming. Several years ago I proposed a scheme for doing precisely this: what I then rather clumsily termed the 'positively discriminating voucher' (PDV) (Le Grand 1989). James O'Shaughnessy and Charlotte Leslie of the think tank Policy Exchange have labelled a version of the idea an 'advantage premium' (O'Shaughnessy and Leslie 2005). Although this is a definite improvement on PDV, it does not seem quite right: 'disadvantage premium' would seem to be more accurate, and so I am relabelling it accordingly.

Under the PDV, or disadvantage premium, scheme, schools that accepted children from poorer areas would receive an extra amount per child: a premium. This would create a positive incentive for schools to take them in. Schools that contained a high proportion of children from poor families would then have more resources per pupil on average than those with a low proportion. They would also have better premises and equipment and could attract higher-quality staff. The outcome would be either selective schools, with those that specialized in the education of the children of the poor being better equipped and staffed than those that specialized in the education of the children of the rich, or, if head teachers or staff did not want to engage in such specializations, schools that contained a reasonable proportion of children from all parts of the social spectrum. One way or another, cream-skimming that favoured the better off would be reduced or eliminated.

It should be noted that this idea is different from an apparently similar scheme in which the funding formulae for state schools in poor areas means that these schools automatically receive an extra amount per child over and above the standard amount received per child. For that 'premium' is generally related to the location of the school, not to the background of the child. Hence schools face no particular incentive to take in children from poor backgrounds; for whatever child they accept they still receive the same amount.

A difficulty with the disadvantage premium or PDV is that it would be necessary to find some way of identifying poor families. This could be done by means tests; but these have well-known difficulties, including administrative complexity and stigmatizing effects. An alternative would be simply to give larger vouchers to families who lived in poorer areas. Many countries have various classification schemes for determining the wealth of areas, including some that are broken down to very small units, such as postcodes.

An example of how this could be applied would be to use the leading form of postcode classification in the United Kingdom: 'Mosaic'. This classifies the 1.3 million postcodes into which the Post Office divides Britain's residential addresses into a set of sixty-one distinct types of residential neighbourhoods. The object of the classification is to define types of residential neighbourhood which are different from each other in terms of the types of people who live in them, in terms of culture, shared experience, aspirations, income, consumption characteristics and level of need for and use of public services. Unpublished work by Dr Foster Research indicates that the Mosaic classification is a very good predictor of educational performance and hence of educational need. This in turn could be used to assess the amount of money needed to help children from less-advantaged backgrounds, and so determine the size of the disadvantage premium.

Variants of this idea have been proposed. The Policy Exchange idea is to attach extra funding to a pupil from a failed school if new management takes over the school or if he or she goes to another school. The premium would be worth £5,000 in the first year but would taper off to zero at the end of four years. If some schools were oversubscribed with advantage-premium children, to avoid cream-skimming they could only select by lottery (O'Shaughnessy and Leslie 2005).

Samuel Bowles and Herbert Gintis have proposed another variant (Bowles and Gintis 1998). This would make the value of the voucher dependent not only on the socio-economic status of the family but also on the socio-economic composition of the school. Thus a voucher presented by a low-income pupil to a school with predominantly high-income pupils would be worth more, giving the school an incentive to attract such pupils. Similarly, a voucher presented by a high-income pupil to a school with predominantly low-income pupils would also be worth more, again giving an incentive to the school to attract such pupils.

David Chater and I (Chater and Le Grand 2006) have proposed applying the idea specifically to looked-after children (previously known as children in care). These children are in many respects the most disadvantaged of all in terms of background, a phenomenon that manifests itself in, among many indicators of dysfunction, very poor educational outcomes. Schools are often reluctant to admit these children and/or to retain them once they are admitted.

The Chater and Le Grand proposal is for a highly visible, additional premium to be attached to looked-after children of school age. This would be payable on a term-by-term basis and would be held by a named, lead professional, a 'corporate parent', on behalf of the child and, where appropriate, their carer. Such a premium would provide schools with an immediate, visible incentive for accepting looked-after children—and, crucially, for keeping them in school. It would also give the lead professional greater control over the education each child receives. Finally, by requiring a named individual to control the premium budget, it would also clearly allocate corporate parenting responsibilities in choosing schools, appealing negative decisions and liaising with teachers.

The Social Care Practice[6]

As noted above, the history of child-based social care in the United Kingdom is a history of poor outcomes, especially for looked-after children. Yet in general the social workers who deal with looked-after children come to the work with a moral purpose, with idealism, energy, enthusiasm and a commitment to rectifying injustice. The persistence of the poor outcome statistics suggests that the aggregate failure to improve outcomes significantly is less likely to be the result of individual failures of individual workers with individual children than it is to be due to a wider malaise.

The fundamental problem is a lack of continuity. In most areas, there is such a rapid turnover of staff that looked-after children are lucky if they have the same social worker for a few months—let alone for the many years necessary to build up the requisite degrees of trust, affection and

[6]This idea was developed independently by myself and by Alistair Pettigrew, Director of Children's Services in Lewisham, and he and I have subsequently worked together to develop the proposal. This section is based on an article that he and I wrote for *The Guardian* and I am very grateful to him for allowing me to use some of that material here.

concern. In addition, local government hierarchies have too many people involved in decision making, most of whom do not have a personal knowledge of the child but rely on the descriptions of others or on written reports. The social worker is then left to convey and to represent decisions to a young person that they may not have personally advocated. In consequence, there is an absence both of effective authority and of a sense of responsibility.

Social workers need to have the authority to make decisions and see them implemented. This means giving them the capacity to secure, on behalf of a looked-after child, high-quality health and education, regular family and peer contact (if appropriate) and choice of appropriate placement. In short, they need to be a caring, responsible 'parent'.

So how can this be achieved? One idea involves the setting up of social care practices or partnerships along the lines of medical or legal practices. This would be a group of perhaps eight to ten professionals (social workers and community workers) who would both provide services themselves and, under contract from the local government, control a commissioning budget. The budget would be based on capitation, with a fixed amount for each child on the practice's list. This budget could be spent on ensuring that the needs of the looked-after child are met. These needs could include normal developmental opportunities, health surveillance and treatment, additional educational support, psychological therapy, appropriate contact with parents and siblings and the wider family. All this would be organized and delivered by the practice professionals themselves to the children on their list, or by spending some of the budget on commissioning specialist care as needed from provider agencies.

The caseload of each worker in the practice would need to be small enough to ensure that the worker had sufficient time to develop a relationship of trust and confidence with the child so that she was able to ensure that she adequately understood the child's needs and enabled the child to be fully involved in all the dimensions of the assessment framework.

The social care practice or partnership could be organized as a non-profit social enterprise, or as a professional partnership (as with GPs in the British NHS). The social workers who are the partners in these organizations would be investing their personal time and resources both in the local community and in the looked-after children themselves. As in equivalent practices in the legal and medical sectors, partners will have different skills and experience. What is important is the creation of a mutually dependent team in which a choice of social worker can be offered to young people in care, a choice that will be made in the knowledge that the social worker selected will be committed for the long term, not just because of the commitment to the young person but because of the worker's commitment to the practice of which they are a member.

This proposal has a number of advantages. Chief among them is that it would encourage continuity of care. Because they would 'own' the business, have a share in its assets and have much greater powers and responsibilities within it, social workers would have a strong incentive to stay in the area, and hence to stay with their client children and families. This contrasts with current practice where, especially in urban conurbations, social workers move from local authority to local authority (or out of social work altogether) as they seek to improve their remuneration and job satisfaction. These job changes have a detrimental effect on looked-after children, as they have had to invest a level of trust in the social worker, who they see as the major decision maker in their life. These young people have already had to come to terms with the loss of other significant adults in their lives. We need to try to ensure that the state does not compound the young person's potential attachment problems through its inaction in addressing the issue of social worker turnover.

Additionally, the partners would also have a strong incentive to do as effective and efficient a job as possible; for in that way they could generate a surplus on their budget that they could spend either on themselves, on improving their facilities or on hiring more staff. And the empowerment involved in the practice idea would in the longer term make social work a more attractive career, and could reverse its long-term decline as a profession.

With the social care practice, all funding streams would be merged into one budget. The members of the practice would have responsibility for the package of overall care provision for their clients. Being relatively small, they would have personal knowledge of and long-term contacts with their clients. They would be separated from specialist provider interests, and hence would be less subject to provider pressure. And they would have an incentive to provide preventive care and to economize on treatment.

In a social care practice world, local government would still have an important role. They would have to specify the budgets for the practices. And they would have to monitor the quality of the service being provided. But that monitoring would be on the outcomes of the process: the welfare of the looked-after children. This would be in sharp contrast to the current system, where micro-management through bureaucratic hierarchies both diffuses responsibility and demotivates front-line workers.

This idea has been taken up by the British government in a recent green paper on looked-after children (Department for Education and Skills 2006a). But there are many issues that need to be resolved before such an idea becomes practical policy. In particular the issues of legal accountability for children taken into care and of how the associated responsibilities are divided between the local authority and the practice are crucial. However, if these concerns can be resolved, the idea has great potential. As professionals trusted with a budget, the social workers involved in social care practices would be empowered and energized. They would provide a more effective and efficient service. But, most importantly, they would provide a caring environment for looked-after children, far superior to that provided under the present system. The consequence would be happier children, growing up into more secure and more confident adults—and more fulfilled social workers.

Conclusion

All of the ideas discussed in this chapter are at a relatively early stage of development. However, the intention was not to present fully formed policies at this stage, but to indicate how some of the more general ideas in this book concerning choice and competition could be developed into specific policy proposals. I hope that enough has been said to indicate their potential.

CHAPTER SIX

The Politics of Choice

The politics of choice and competition in public services are complex. The issues involved do not fit neatly into the boxes of left or right, of social democrat, socialist, conservative or liberal. On the contrary, political parties of whatever stripe are generally divided over the policies concerned, with influential groups within each party pulling in opposite directions. Even those directly involved, including both providers and users, are often unclear about the relevant arguments and, in consequence, where they stand on the issue.

In this chapter I review some of these tensions. I consider two kinds of interest group: ideological and functional. The ideological groups are the social democratic left and the conservative right.[1] The functional groups can

---

[1] I have had difficulty in deciding upon the appropriate terms here. There are a proliferation of possible labels for what used to be known as the left or centre-left including social democratic, new Labour, progressive and (in US terminology) liberal. Similarly, on the right or centre-right, as well as old-style conservatives there are christian democrats, neo-liberals and neo-conservatives. In what follows, I have used the terms social democratic left broadly to include progressives, new Labour and of course social democrats (and even socialists), and conservatives to include all the

also be split into two: those who work in the public sector, providers, and those who benefit from it, users or potential users.

Of course, these groupings are not mutually exclusive. Most of those who work in the public sector also use it, whether as parents of children at state or government schools or as patients in the publicly funded health services. Both social democrats and conservatives can be found working in the public sector (although probably more of the former than the latter); and of course most will also use it (although again probably more of the former than the latter). Even the political divide between the social democrat and the conservative can be crossed, as indeed I hope to show in what follows. Nonetheless, it is worth distinguishing between the groups, for they do have different interests and concerns; and individuals articulating those concerns in the political arena will behave differently according to which role he or she identifies with at the time.

Most of the political tensions surrounding the issues centre on the competing merits and demerits of the four models for delivering public services that we have been considering in this book, so it might be as well to remind the reader what they are. The first is the *trust model*, where professionals and managers are simply trusted to know what is best for their users and to deliver high-quality services without interference from government or any other source. Then there is the opposite of trust: the version of command-and-control that we have termed the

equivalents on the right. Although inevitably this involves some drastic oversimplification, there is enough commonality within these groups in their views on the issues discussed here to justify these categorizations.

targets model, where central management sets targets for providers, rewards them if they succeed in meeting those targets and penalizes them if they fail. The third is the *voice model*, where users express their dissatisfaction (or satisfaction) directly to providers through face-to-face conversations, or through complaints to higher managers or elected representatives. And finally there is, of course, the *choice and competition model*, where tax-funded users choose services offered by competing providers.

The Social Democratic Left

Many social democrats are instinctively hostile to choice and competition in public services. This is partly because choice and competition are associated with markets, and for them, markets have almost exclusively negative associations.[2] For the committed social democrat, a market-oriented world is one where uncaring capitalists exploit vulnerable consumers, persuading them to buy superficial trivialities at the expense of the really worthwhile things in life. Not only that, but competing businesses drive down the pay and worsen the conditions of workers, while encouraging them to spend their meagre wages on low-quality goods with high profit margins. The social democrats' fear is that these consequences of the operation of real markets will be replicated in the public service quasi-market, with sick patients in hospitals and vulnerable children in schools left to the tender mercies of

---

[2] I say 'almost' exclusively because, even for social democrats, the term can have positive associations in certain contexts. A 'market town', for instance, is often considered a rather attractive place to live.

ruthless private firms—many of whom will be that modern embodiment of evil, the large US corporation (Pollock 2005).

In fact, of the four models of public service delivery discussed in earlier chapters, the instinct of most social democrats would be to run with the 'trust' model. That is, they would prefer professionals and others who work in the public services to be trusted with service delivery without interference from government or anyone else. This preference arises partly because many social democrats actually work in the public sector; and, unsurprisingly, as we shall see, that is the model preferred by public sector professionals and other workers in the sector. But it also stems from less self-interested concerns: from a widely held belief in both the prevalence and desirability of 'knightly' motivations, or what may be termed more loosely the public service ethos (Le Grand 2003).

More precisely, much social democratic thought is based on the assumption that those who work in the public sector are knights or something close to perfect altruists: to have as their principal concern the welfare of those whom they are supposed to be serving, and not to be motivated to any significant extent by their own personal concerns—as knaves would be (Le Grand 2003). In such a world, public sector professionals can be trusted to get on with the job; they do not have to be told what to do or incentivized in other ways to provide a good service. Indeed the provision of incentives could be counterproductive: treating knightly public servants like knaves may actually turn them into knaves.

Now sophisticated social democrats would acknowledge that, on occasion, even knightly professionals can get it wrong, that some knights may even in reality be

knaves, and that users might not always be satisfied
with the service that they get. Hence they need a second model to supplement the trust model when that goes
awry. But the second model that we have considered
above—targets and performance management—does not,
in general, attract them.[3] They do not like the distortions
that targets create, and they dislike the authoritarianism
implicit in performance management, because, among
other things, it demoralizes the knights.

Of our models this leaves only voice and choice. And
here social democrats would prefer to turn to voice rather
than choice. This is partly again because of their belief in
the fundamental knightliness of public service providers:
all that doctors, nurses, teachers have to do is to be told
that something is not quite right and they will willingly
correct it. But the social democratic preference for voice
may also stem from more self-interested concerns. Many
social democrats are middle class; and, as we saw in earlier chapters in some detail, the middle classes are good at
using voice mechanisms to obtain what they want. Moreover, the middle classes already have choices of a kind.
If dissatisfied with the service they are receiving from the
public sector, they can move house; or they can go private.

In fact, therein lies one of the principal difficulties
for the social democratic position. For the models that
are favoured, especially voice, can violate a fundamental
social democratic principle: that of the promotion of social
justice or equity. Most social democrats have a commitment to high-quality public services delivered equitably—
especially for the less well off. But this conflicts with their

[3]Although some do retain an affection for central planning—a
component of command-and-control.

model preferences. For, as we have demonstrated, there is a respectable case for arguing that voice does not deliver equity, especially when there is the opportunity of going privately. Whereas choice and competition within the public sector can promote equity—so long as the policies are properly designed.

In short, therefore, the social democratic hostility to choice and competition is misplaced. The models it favours (trust and voice) will not generally deliver high-quality, responsive and efficient services; and they will not usually deliver equitable ones. The choice-and-competition model thus can be reconciled with social democratic ideals in that it can deliver on all these dimensions—so long as the policies concerned are properly designed.

The Conservative Right

Fundamentally, the conservative right is more likely to favour choice and competition over other models of public service delivery. Indeed, many of the mechanisms for choice and competition that we have been discussing in previous chapters were introduced into British health care and education by the Conservative government of Margaret Thatcher and John Major.[4]

This commitment to the choice-and-competition model arises partly because, as I have argued elsewhere, the right has beliefs about the motivation of those who work in the public sector that are the polar opposite of those of the social democrat (Le Grand 2003, chapter 1). Public sector professionals and other workers are assumed not to be

---

[4]For a full description of these reforms see Le Grand and Bartlett (1993, chapter 1).

perfect knights, whose only concern is with the welfare of others, but rather knaves: egoists, primarily focused on their own interests. In that world, to serve the public good, they will have to be provided with incentives that appeal to their self-interest. Through Adam Smith's invisible hand, markets are the best way to provide such incentives, or, more generally, the best way to corral self-interest to meet the public interest. Hence any model of public service delivery that incorporates market elements such as user choice and provider competition is likely to be superior to models that do not.

However, even their support for choice and competition operating within a public sector quasi-market is likely to be less than wholehearted. For the question they will always ask is: why is the market 'quasi'? Why not go for a full market? If the aim is to empower users, then why not let them use their own money in deciding how much education or health care to buy? Why should that power be taken away from them by the state through coercive taxation?

But this position too is problematic. If people can use their own money, then the better off will purchase more health care for themselves and their families and better education for their children than the less well off. This creates uneasiness even among those who propound a right-wing philosophy. Much (though not all) ill health arises from factors largely beyond individual control; should the poor be penalized for this in a way that the better off are not? Children are not responsible for their parent's wealth or lack of it: should they have to suffer if their parents do not have the means to purchase them a good education? A full-blooded libertarian might overcome this objection by arguing that the priority of liberty dominates every other consideration, and coercive taxation cannot be justified even for desirable ends such as treating those who are sick through no fault of their own or promoting equality of educational opportunity for all children. But few conservatives are that single-minded in their pursuit of liberty; and the tension between their desire for minimal state intervention and the provision of efficient and equitable public services remains.

Providers

In April 2006, the British Secretary of State for Health, Patricia Hewitt, had to stop a speech she was making at the Annual Conference of the Royal College of Nursing because of the audience's jeers and slow handclaps. The speech ended in confusion with the chairman having to cut it short. The event was described the next day as being part of the worst day that the government of which Ms Hewitt was a part had ever had.

The degree of hostility evinced by the audience's behaviour was puzzling. For, on the face of it, the nursing profession was in better health than ever before in British history. Their numbers had increased dramatically since the government came to power: up by 85,000 since 1997. Entry-level nurses' pay had increased by 25% in real terms; the average cash salary of nurses had increased by around 50%. A nurse consultant grade had been introduced; those promoted to that grade could earn twice the average.

So why was there all the fuss? Partly it arose because at the time there were accumulating stories of hospital deficits and job losses. But even these did not really explain the hostility. The deficits were trivial: less than 1% of total NHS spending and the sort of sum that gets lost in the accounting noise of a large corporation. Moreover, if they were set against an underspend on capital in that year, the NHS as a whole was actually in surplus. The job 'losses' were also tiny relative to the NHS labour force of 1.3 million. And most of them were not in fact real losses. Rather, they were decisions to freeze recruitment to unfilled posts and not to take on more agency staff.

In fact, the resentment had several sources. Partly, it was the process of reform. Many felt, rightly or wrongly, that they had not been consulted about the reforms that the government was introducing, while those who had been consulted felt that their views had not been taken into account. It was also the sheer pace of change. The reforms included the extension of patient choice for elective surgery, a new payment system for hospitals, new forms of provider, including 'foundation' trusts and independent sector treatment and diagnostic centres, a massive IT programme, and badly timed institutional reorganization. All of this happened more or less simultaneously and placed an intolerable strain on many NHS staff.

But the resentment also reflected a general unease about the direction of reform. Medical professionals are brought up to believe that they are entitled to considerable autonomy, not only in clinical matters, but also in organizational ones too. Specialist consultants are used to running their own empires within hospitals. GPs (in Britain at least) are independent business people, controlling their own small enterprises. Even nurses, though less powerful than doctors, have their own areas of power and control, especially where hospital wards are concerned.

But much of this autonomy has been steadily eroded— in England at least. Hospital managers have become more powerful (although they still have a long way to go before they can effectively manage consultants). The imposition of targets and performance management from the top compelled both managers and professionals to confine their activities to what the government wanted, and severely limited their freedom of action in other areas. Even in clinical areas, doctors' prerogatives were being circumscribed by the development of government guidelines over what treatments they can undertake and what medicines they can prescribe.

Targets are now dropping out of fashion in the United Kingdom. But the professionals are faced with what they perceive to be yet another major threat to their power and autonomy: the quasi-market in secondary care (and increasingly in primary care too) that the government is setting up in large part as a substitute for performance management. The expansion of patient choice and increased competition from foundation trusts and from contracts with the independent sector, and the introduction of new providers of GP services all mean that, if organizations are to thrive, there will have to be significant changes in both clinical and organizational behaviour. The discipline of the market is replacing the discipline of targets.

However, from the point of view of medical professionals and indeed the NHS staff as a whole, this change from target to market should be an improvement. As we saw in earlier chapters, a command-and-control regime, where demanding targets are combined with heavy, top-down performance management, is demotivating and demoralizing. It offers less freedom of action than does operation as an autonomous agent in a market context: much less scope for initiative and much more being told what to do.

The downside, of course, is that with this greater freedom may come less security. However, this should not be overplayed. People lose their jobs in command-and-control systems, often with less opportunity of re-employment than markets offer. Also, in a world with a shortage of doctors and nurses, it is very unlikely that any medical professional who loses their job in the event that their hospital or GP practice closes would remain unemployed for long.

More generally, of all our models, public sector professionals and managers would obviously prefer the trust model. No professional enjoys being told what to do—by government or by users. But if the trust model is not on offer, then it seems reasonable to suppose that professionals would far prefer to work in the context of a quasi-market than under the dead hand of command-and-control. Perhaps, when NHS nurses have experienced the greater freedoms of the market (which, at the time of writing, most have yet to do), they will agree.

Users

Chapter 2 examined the views of users concerning choice in some detail and there is relatively little to add here. As we saw there, the majority of users do appear to want choice in public services—especially, and perhaps surprisingly, the less powerful or less well off. However, those who claim to represent users do not always agree. The British Consumers' Association, for instance, seems opposed to the extension of user choice in the public sector. Its report on choice that we referred to in an earlier chapter is almost unremittingly hostile to the idea, concentrating on spelling out the problems with choice and competition and expressing scepticism that greater choice can deliver the benefits its advocates claim (*Which?* 2005). This is slightly puzzling; but perhaps it can be explained by the fact that most consumer bodies are resolutely middle class and that both their writers and readers can already obtain what they want from the public sector without needing any extension of choice to the less fortunate.

The interests of users, especially those from disadvantaged backgrounds, often get lost in the heat of political debate. This is undesirable not only from the perspective of the wider society but also from the perspective of the political system. For a public service is designed to give a good service to the public, and at the end of the day it is only the public that can decide whether it is successfully doing that.

Conclusion

Despite their popularity with users (if not with some of those who speak for users), policies designed to introduce user choice and provider competition have relatively few friends in the political world. The social democratic left instinctively dislikes them. The more conservative or liberal right thinks they are still part of the apparatus of the big government and nanny state that they detest. Providers hate the loss of power implicit in user choice, and the insecurity associated with competition.

Yet they offer benefits to all these groups. Properly designed, the policies concerned can meet social democratic aims, such as equity and social justice, and do so better than the alternatives, such as voice. They can deliver efficient and non-paternalistic social services, thus avoiding the criticisms of government waste and excessive dirigisme that characterize conservatives' criticisms of the welfare state. In quasi-market systems, providers have a freedom to act and to innovate in a way that other models do not allow, especially models that involve targets and performance management. And through the extension of choice for users they can deliver a higher quality, more responsive service than the other models are able to.

And it is in a comparison with the alternative models that the essence of the political argument lies. The task for governments committed to choice-and-competition policies, and the task for those who advise them, is to use theory and evidence to demonstrate to all the interest groups involved, not that these policies will deliver perfect services, but that they will generally provide a higher quality, more responsive, more efficient and more equitable service than the alternatives. It is hoped that this book can contribute to that demonstration.

Afterwords

An American Perspective
By Alain Enthoven[1]

Beyond sharing a common language, democracy and the rule of law, American and British people also share frustration about the performance of their public services, particularly elementary and secondary education and medical care. The problems in medical care are somewhat different on the two sides of the Atlantic. American Medicare and Medicaid spending is running out of control, whereas the British NHS has spending under much better control. But people in both countries have good reason to be concerned about the quality of health services, as well as their accountability and responsiveness. We have similar problems in education: too many children leaving school without the skills needed to function effectively in the twenty-first century global economy.

A prominent public opinion poll in the United Kingdom asked people what words they think apply to British public services today. Respondents most frequently said 'bureaucratic', 'infuriating', 'faceless', 'hard working', 'unresponsive' and 'unaccountable'. Least frequently, they said 'friendly', 'efficient', 'honest and open'. I would not be surprised to read of a similar result in the United States. In fact, the daily battles over school choice

[1]Marriner S. Eccles Professor of Public and Private Management (Emeritus) in the Graduate School of Business, Stanford University.

and the enactment of the No Child Left Behind Act in America attest to the fact that most Americans believe their schools are not producing the results they should.

Julian Le Grand, an eminent British economist, professor at the London School of Economics and sometime advisor to Prime Minister Tony Blair, has written an analysis of the various means of social control that can be used to elicit better performance in public services. The goals are to achieve high quality, efficiency or good value for money, responsiveness, accountability and equity. The means include the following.

- Trusting the professionals (doctors, nurses, teachers) to act to achieve these goals.

- What Americans are likely to call 'top down command and control' and what the British are more likely to call 'targets and performance management'.

- What Hirschman has called 'voice', that is, attempts to change an unsatisfactory state of affairs by organizing and attending protest meetings and mobilizing public opinion.

- Choice and competition, that is, giving consumers or patients choices and thereby giving providers incentives to satisfy consumers.

Le Grand's analysis explains the considerations that led Prime Minister Tony Blair to respond to rising dissatisfaction with public services by moving the traditionally 'command and control' oriented Labour party to less emphasis on performance management or targets, and to a greater emphasis on consumer choice and competition. He argues persuasively that nonchoice systems can favour the better off. For example, 'Generally, middle class patients and parents are more articulate, more confident and more persistent than their poorer equivalents.' On the other hand, schools and clinics will compete actively to serve and satisfy poor people if government arms them with the requisite purchasing power.

Le Grand's analysis should be of great interest to American readers because we, in America, are facing large public policy issues in which these questions are central. For example, Republicans and centrist Democrats favour school choice, while more 'liberal' (in the American sense of the term) Democrats oppose it, preferring to rely on trust and voice. The teachers' unions are large supporters of the Democratic Party, and teachers, understandably, strongly prefer the trust model. Le Grand reviews American experience with school choice in Milwaukee and Florida, as well as studies of school choice experience by Harvard economist Caroline Hoxby.

Medicare, the US Federal Government programme of health insurance for the aged and disabled, is on a trajectory that will make it unaffordable, so fundamental reform will be unavoidable. Medicare was based on the trust model, but with a fee-for-service payment system that includes strong incentives for doctors to do more when less would produce the same health outcome. It has become increasingly clear that Medicare pays more for bad doctors than for good ones, because if doctors' mistakes cause complications, or if they fail to diagnose and prescribe correctly, Medicare pays them to fix the problems they created. Republicans and centrist Democrats generally favour solutions that increase choice and competition. Their idea is to let alternatives to this defective payment system emerge and evolve to the point of replacing fee-for-service. Consumers seeking value for money would choose them. Other more traditional Democrats prefer solutions that rely more completely on collective action and the government dictating the choices. For example, Congress, while under Republican control, enacted a model of prescription drug coverage for Medicare beneficiaries that relies on competition in the private sector. The Democratic leadership favours a model in which the government does the negotiating for prices with the drug companies. Their logic would eventually lead to the end of the choice and competition model in Medicare drugs.

'Single payer' proposals (i.e. systems of payment that resemble the Canadian model or American Medicare), often favoured by the left in American politics, would rely mainly on fee-for-service with its expenditure-increasing incentives, thus producing a financially unsustainable result that would force the creation of more and more government 'command and control' such as controls on facilities construction, medical practice and, finally, 'global budgets' on hospitals. The Canadian and British experience with global budgets is not positive. In that model, there is no incentive to improve efficiency and treat more patients, with the inevitable result of longer waiting lines. So the Blair government is moving to more competition and choice to motivate efficiency improvement.

Some people have an overly simplistic idea of what competition is. So Le Grand explains some of the conditions that must be met for 'competition' to produce the desired incentives and improvements. First, competition must be real. That is, there need to be actual and potential competitors. But it is not enough for there to be choice. As Margaret Thatcher famously said when introducing the 'internal market' model in the NHS, 'money follows patients'. Schools and hospitals that attract more pupils and patients must receive correspondingly more resources to care for them. Alternatives must be available, which might mean, in the British context, providing transportation to low-income patients and their families if they want to travel to a more distant hospital for better or more convenient care. And choice must be informed by indicators of quality of services. The Patient Care Advisor (PCA) piloted in the United Kingdom could help with this. And cream skimming must be avoided. For example, American health insurers compete by attracting healthy patients who are unlikely to need medical care and avoiding patients likely to need it. Schools can ease their workload and report better results by attracting more talented and better-prepared students. Le Grand describes several ways of managing this problem, including risk-adjusting the tariff system such that higher-risk patients or students have a higher tariff, paid by government, associated with them. The Dutch, who do this in their health insurance system, call it 'risk equalization'.

The book is written in a clear accessible style, meant for the interested general reader and not just for other economists. It is a very interesting story, how and why the 'command and control' oriented Labour Party chose to move to consumer choice and competition models. I hope that more Democrats in America will read this book and move toward similar views. Republicans who prefer choice and competition will be aided in their ability to explain and make their case.

A Sceptic's Perspective
By David Lipsey[2]

As a politician-turned-journalist-turned-politician I am a trained killer controversialist. My first instinct is to run direct at the opposition with head down and horns sharpened. I expected to play that role when Julian Le Grand asked me to contribute a commentary to his new book on choice in public services, something about which I have been privately and publicly critical.

But I cannot. I hope it is not just the clarity of Le Grand's argument and the breadth of his evidence that has weakened me as the banderillero weakens the bull. Headlong charge against this remarkable volume is not possible.

For I agree with Le Grand that the three traditional ways of making public services work—trusting professionals, pressure through voice, and command-and-control through targets—are (jointly and severally) not enough. I agree with him that choice and competition also have a part to play. And most of all, I agree with him that a mixture of all these elements is necessary; and that it is crucial to find the right balance between them. Where, however, our emphasis remains different is that he is (as both an academic and a practical adviser to government) a passionate advocate for choice, while I am more sceptical.

I am sceptical about choice in the private sector, as well as the public. The weakest of all arguments for more choice in the public sector is that, because people have it when they shop in Tesco, they should have it for schools and hospitals. In fact, as the American academic Barry Schwartz shows, in his polemic *The Paradox of Choice*, choice for

[2]Lord David Lipsey is a Labour peer and Chair of the Social Market Foundation.

consumers is often a cause of bewilderment and dissatisfaction. Schwartz cites evidence that shows, for example, that when people are offered a few jams to taste, most make a purchase, but offered thirty or more, most do not.

If I were to identify a single cause of the malaise of the modern West, it would be this. Ours is, as Anthony Giddens has pointed out, the first generation to view life other than the playing out of fate. However, we have gone too far the other way, believing that we can enjoy autonomy in everything. In fact, choice is expensive (since it requires research into information) and often disappointing (we feel angrier when a choice does not work out than when we suffer a quirk of fate).

There are two key arguments for choice. One is the libertarian one: that it is a good in itself, gives people pleasure and makes them happier. The other is an instrumental one: that choice is a way of improving efficiency and encouraging innovation. These two arguments can be applied in the public as well as the private sector. I am much more sympathetic to the instrumental than to the libertarian argument; and favour those extensions of choice based on it, rather than on libertarian arguments.

The opponents of choice in public services often use bad arguments. For example, in a mysterious book, the political philosopher David Marquand seemed to argue that some things are intrinsically public, and perhaps morally superior as a result. At the other end of the spectrum, a powerful trade union alliance has formed which ostensibly is arguing for the protection of public services, but in practice is arguing for the interests of the workers who supply them. Le Grand gives such feeble arguments short shrift. However, although he fairly addresses an argument I have previously developed about the flaws of choice

('Too much choice', *Prospect*, December 2005), he does not give it the weight it deserves.

In general I am suspicious of analogies with the public sector drawn from the workings of the market sector of the economy. True, the market sector features choice, but not unconstrained choice. Consumers in the market place face a budget constraint—their income—and a set of prices. Individuals getting services in the public sector face no such budget constraint. They are free to demand more of everything—meanwhile, if they wish, resisting any tax increases to pay for the everything. Given this, market arguments do not directly apply to the public sector; and the workings of Adam Smith's invisible hand are therefore very different.

More specifically, there are three flaws from economic theory in the choice model. They are externalities (that choices may involve high costs or benefits to those not making them), agency (that the choice model only works if the choice is made by people for themselves) and the costs of information. Le Grand does not explicitly reject these but he does not think them very important.

An example drawn from this book demonstrates otherwise. Le Grand points out that both the middle classes and the working classes want choice in education. The question then is: do they have use that choice with different objectives? For example, the middle class might want their kids to achieve; the working class want them to be happy at school. Or the middle class might be prepared (coming from two-car households) to transport their kids further than the no- or one-car working class household in search of a better school.

Le Grand agrees that there is 'remarkably little' evidence about the criteria that parents use in making their

choice. He does cite one study by Anne West and her colleagues at the LSE that suggests only quite modest class
differences in the desire of parents for their children to go
into further education. However, it remains the case that
middle class children already tend to end up at higher-
performing schools than working class children, and it is
at least possible that expanded choice would exacerbate
this differential.

Now this shows two of the economic flaws in the choice
model acutely. It raises the problem of externalities. In
making their choice, the working class parent inflicts two
external costs on society: a lower GDP (since they will
not achieve as much in the world of work) and less social
mobility (since their kids will not aspire to middle class
positions). As for agency, this too is dubious since people
are deciding for their children. Middle class parents may
subject their children to the mental and physical torture
called 'boarding school' in the hope that this will mean
they emerge equipped to become rich enough to sustain
them in their old age.

Information is a further cost. If people are sick, do they
really want to spend their days scouring lists of consultants trying to find out which one is least likely to kill
them on the operating table? Especially when the information is complex, and often inadequate? For example,
any surgeon can optimize his record by refusing to operate on the sickest patients. Yes it is true that patients can
be equipped with choice advisers to assist them (actually
these have always existed but they used to be called GPs).
That may reduce the cost of information to the patient
but it is an additional cost that society as a whole has to
bear. And, as Schwartz reports, American research shows
that 65% of people say they would want to choose their

treatment if they got cancer but only 12% of actual cancer patients said they wanted the same freedom.

Finally, and this is the most contentious bit of the argument, there is the issue from equity. Public services, so it is argued, are public services largely because we want them to be more equally distributed than is income generally. We do not mind if plutocrat A can eat more caviar than binman B, but we do expect the latter to get (at least) nearly as much health care. However, if choice is introduced, many fear, the middle classes will be assisted in their quest to ensure that they get the lion's share of public services, as they do of private goods.

Now, this argument is often exaggerated by the critics of choice. They assume that public services are egalitarian without properly examining the evidence; for the evidence suggests (for health care, for education) that the sharp middle class elbows are working pretty well under the supposedly equitable system we have. For a more balanced judgement, one has to examine the evidence, such as it is. Will the introduction of choice and competition in this sector add to or reduce inequality of provision? If it will reduce it, is that a price worth paying for greater efficiency and for maintaining a wide base of political support for good public services?

In theory there are mechanisms which could correct for any new inequalities created. For example, Le Grand floats a scheme for looked-after children (those who used to be called children in care) whereby schools that admitted them would get more public cash. I applaud this in principle, though I have my political doubts: in general, positive discrimination in the use of the state's cash tends not to prove popular with voters.

In this as in other items on the 'choice and competition' agenda, in practice, what seems sensible is a policy of cautious experimentation, constant piloting and careful, scrupulous research. I rather expect more choice to have an inegalitarian effect in education, and therefore, wearing my theoretical rather than my political hat, I applaud Brighton's experiment with allocating school places by lot as an imaginative way of dealing with this problem. I think that direct payments work well in long-term care, that choice of GP could improve primary care but that choice will work badly for elective surgery. These are but one man's more-or-less-informed prejudices. Only time and trial will tell.

Meanwhile, the proponents of choice should continue to be robust in attacking the sillier arguments of their opponents; while remaining modest in their claims of what their policy would achieve. The current government is in danger of spoiling its public sector reform efforts by portraying them as a crusade, sallying into unexplored territory without proper caution and well-plotted maps. Julian Le Grand served as a senior adviser to Tony Blair, and I feel certain that his memos to the boss were couched in the judicious language he uses in this book. If so it is not his fault that the messianic tendencies of this government are in danger of ruining a set of policies that has much to offer but is no panacea.

Further Reading

Much of the literature in this area takes the form of articles, the most relevant of which are listed in the bibliography. Here we list a few of the key books and monographs that might help the reader who wishes to pursue some of the arguments in this book.

Some of the general principles and analysis underlying the book's thesis can be found in Le Grand (2003). Important precursors of that book (and hence of this one) include Schultze (1977) and Pinker (1971, 1979).

There are few general works specifically on choice and competition. Exceptions are Lent and Arend (2004), which usefully summarizes the principal arguments for and against choice and competition, and Prabhakar (2006), which includes a helpful discussion of alternative forms of organization engaged in public service delivery.

For those interested in the United Kingdom government's general approach to public service reform, PMSU (2006b) has a good overview. A useful critique of that approach is the House of Commons Public Administration Select Committee Report (2005).

On health care, the place to begin is the work of the pioneer on market-oriented reforms of state systems such as the British NHS: Alain Enthoven (1985, 1999, 2002). As noted in the main text, Propper et al. (2006) and Fotaki et al. (2006) review the evidence on the impact of choice and competition. Gaynor (2006) and Van Beusekon et al. (2004)

are good places to find evidence concerning the United States, and what little evidence there is from Europe can be found in Dixon and Thomson (2006). Farrington-Douglas and Allen (2005) provides a comprehensive overview of the issues concerning equity and choice. Spiers (2003) covers similar ground to parts of this book and is a good provocative read on the topic. Good discussions of the arguments and evidence concerning privatization of the public sector generally can be found in Vickers and Yarrow (1988), and of hospitals in particular in Preker and Harding (2002). For an alternative view, see Pollock (2005).

Gorard et al. (2003) provides an excellent overview of the debates on choice in education. Williams and Rossiter (2004), PMSU (2006a) and Burgess et al. (2005) summarize the evidence on school choice. Wood (2005) discusses the issues involved in secondary-school choice. For an alternative view of the arguments in this book, see Crouch (2003).

Bibliography

Abildgaard, J., and T. Vad. 2003. Can vouchers work for health? The Scandinavian experience. *Progressive Politics* 2:35–40.

Alvarez-Rosete, A., G. Bevan, N. Mays and J. Dixon. 2005. Effect of diverging policy across the NHS. *British Medical Journal* 331:946–50.

Anderson, R., and D. Anderson. 1999. The cost-effectiveness of home birth. *Journal of Nurse-Midwifery* 44:30–35.

Appleby, J., and A. Alvarez-Rosete. 2005. Public response to NHS reform. In *The British Social Attitudes Survey, 22nd Report*. London: Sage.

Appleby, J., A. Harrison and N. Devlin. 2003. *What Is the Real Cost of More Patient Choice?* London: Kings Fund.

Audit Commission. 2004. *Choice in Public Services*. London: Audit Commission.

Auditor General for Wales. 2005. *NHS Waiting Times for Wales. Volume 2: Tackling the Problem*. Cardiff: National Audit Office Wales.

Bergström, F., and M. Sandstrom. 2002. School vouchers in practice: competition won't hurt you. Working Paper 578(2002), Research Institute of Industrial Economics (IUI), Stockholm.

Bevan, G., and C. Hood. 2006. Have targets improved performance in the English NHS? *British Medical Journal* 332: 419–22.

———. Forthcoming. What's measured is what matters: targets and gaming in the English public health care system. *Public Administration*.

Bositis, D. 1999. *National Opinion Poll—Education 1999*. Washington, DC: Joint Center for Political and Economic Studies.

Bowles, S., and H. Gintis. 1998. Efficient redistribution: new rules for markets, states and communities, In *Recasting Egalitarianism: New Rules for Communities, States and Markets* (ed. E. Olin Wright). London: Verso.

Bradley, S., and J. Taylor. 2002. The effect of the quasi-market on the efficiency–equity trade-off in the secondary school sector. *Bulletin of Economic Research* 54:295–314.

Bradley, S., G. Johnes and J. Millington. 2001. The effect of competition on the efficiency of secondary schools in England. *European Journal of Operational Research* 135:545–68.

Burgess, S., and A. Briggs. 2006. School assignment, school choice and social mobility. Centre for Market and Public Organisation, Discussion Paper DP 06/157. University of Bristol.

Burgess, S., C. Propper and D. Wilson. 2005. *Will More Choice Improve Outcomes in Education and Health Care? The Evidence from Economic Research*. University of Bristol: The Centre for Market and Public Organisation.

Burgess, S., B. McConell, C. Propper and D. Wilson. 2007. The impact of school choice on sorting by ability and socio-economic factors in English secondary education. In *Schools and the Equal Opportunity Problem* (ed. L. Woessman and P. Peterson). Cambridge, MA: MIT Press.

Caton, H. 2006. The flat-pack patient? Creating health together. *Patient Education and Counseling* 62:288–89.

Centre for Economic Performance. 2006. *The Depression Report*. London School of Economics.

Chamberlain, T., S. Rutt and F. Fletcher-Campbell. 2006. *Admissions: Who Goes Where? Messages from Statistics*. Slough: National Foundation for Educational Research.

Chater, D., and J. Le Grand. 2006. *Looked After or Overlooked? Good Parenting and School Choice for Looked After Children*. London: Social Market Foundation.

Coast, J. 2001. Who wants to know if their care is rationed? Views of citizens and service informants. *Health Expectations* 4:243–52.

Coulter, A. 2002. *The Autonomous Patient: Ending Paternalism in Medical Care.* London: The Nuffield Trust.

Coulter, A., N. Le Maistre and L. Henderson. 2005. *Patients' Experience of Choosing where to Undergo Surgical Treatment— Evaluation of the London Patient Choice Scheme.* Oxford: Picker Institute.

Crilly, T., and J. Le Grand. 2004. The motivation and behaviour of hospital trusts. *Social Science and Medicine* 58:1809–23.

Crouch, C. 2003. *Commercialisation or Citizenship: Education Policy and the Future of Public Services.* London: Fabian Society.

Cullen, J. B., B. Jacob and S. Levitt. 2000. The impact of school choice on student outcomes: an analysis of the Chicago public schools. NBER Working Paper 7888, National Bureau of Economic Research, Cambridge, MA.

Dale, S., R. Brown, B. Phillips, J. Schore and B. Lepidus Carlson. 2003. The effects of cash and counseling on personal care services and Medicaid costs in Arkansas. *Health Affairs* November:566–75.

Damiani, M., J. Dixon and C. Propper. 2005. Mapping choice in the NHS: cross-sectional study of analysis of routinely collected data. *British Medical Journal* 330:284.

Dawson, D., R. Jacobs, S. Martin and P. Smith. 2004. Evaluation of the London Patient Choice Project: system-wide impacts. Final Report. Report by the Centre for Health Economics, University of York.

Denham, C., and I. White. 1998. Difference in urban and rural Britain. *Population Trends* 91:23–34.

Department for Education and Skills. 2001. *Statistics of Education: Public Examinations GCSE/GNVQ and GCE/AGNVQ in England 2000.* London: Department for Education and Skills (see www.dfes.gov.uk / rsgateway / DB / VOL / v000279 / vol02-2001.pdf).

Department for Education and Skills. 2005. *Higher Standards: Better Schools for All. More Choice for Parents and Pupils* (CM 6677). London: TSO.

———. 2006a. *Care Matters: Transforming Lives of Children and Young People in Care* (CM 6932). London: TSO.

———. 2006b. *GCSE and Equivalent Results and Associated Value Added Measures in England, 2004/05 (Final)*. London: Department for Education and Skills (see www.dfes.gov.uk/rsgateway/DB/SFR/s000664).

Department of Health. 2003. *Building on the Best: Choice, Responsiveness and Equity in the NHS*. London: TSO.

———. 2005a. *Chief Executive's Report to the NHS: December 2005*. London: Department of Health.

———. 2005b. *Expert Patients Programme: Internal Evaluation*. London: Department of Health (see www.expertpatients.nhs.uk / public / cms / uploads / evaluation%20headlines %20140605%20final.pdf).

———. 2005c. *Independence, Well-Being and Choice: Our Vision for the Future of Adult Social Care in England. The Social Care Green Paper*. London: TSO.

———. 2006. *Better Care for Patients: ISTCs—The Story So Far*. London: Department of Health.

Diamond, P. 2006. *Efficiency, Public Virtue and the Delivery of World-Class Public Services*. London: Policy Network.

Disney, R., J. Haskel and Y. Heden. 2003. Restructuring and productivity growth in UK manufacturing. *Economic Journal* 113:666–94.

Dixon, A., and J. Le Grand. 2006. Is greater patient choice consistent with equity? The case of the English NHS. *Journal of Health Services Research and Policy* 11:162–66.

Dixon, A., and S. Thomson. 2006. Choices in health care: the European experience. *Journal of Health Services Research and Policy* 11:167–71.

Dixon, A., J. Le Grand, J. Henderson, R. Murray and E. Poliakoff. 2003. Is the NHS equitable? LSE Health and Social Care Discussion Paper 11, London School of Economics.

Dixon, A., J. Le Grand, J. Henderson, R. Murray and E. Poli-akoff. Forthcoming. Is the British National Health Service equitable? The evidence on socio-economic differences in utilisation. *Journal of Health Services Research and Policy*, in press.

Enthoven, A. C. 1985. *Reflections on the Management of the National Health Service: An American Looks at Incentives to Efficiency in Health Services Management in the UK*. London: Nuffield Provincial Hospitals Trust.

———. 1999. *In Pursuit of an Improving National Health Service*. London: The Nuffield Trust.

———. 2002 *Introducing Market Forces into Health Care: A Tale of Two Countries*. London: The Nuffield Trust.

———. 2006. Connecting consumer choice to the healthcare system. *Journal of Health Law* 39:289–305.

Farrington-Douglas, J., and J. Allen. 2005. *Equitable Choices*. London: Institute for Public Policy Research.

Fiske, E. B., and H. F. Ladd. 2000. *When Schools Compete: A Cautionary Tale*. Washington, DC: Brookings Institute Press.

Foster, L., R. Brown, B. Phillips, J. Schore and B. Lepidus Carlson. 2003. Improving the quality of Medicaid personal assistance through consumer direction. *Health Affairs* (web exclusive) W3:162–75 (see http://content.healthaffairs.org /cgi/reprint/hlthaff.w3.162v1.pdf, accessed 28 September 2006).

Fotaki, M., A. Boyd, L. Smith, R. McDonald, A. Edwards, G. Elwyn, M. Roland and R. Sheaff. 2006. *Patient Choice and the Organisation and Delivery of Health Services: Scoping Review*. Report for the National Co-ordinating Centre for NHS Service Delivery Organisation (NCCSDO). London: SDO.

Gaynor, M. 2006. What do we know about competition and quality in health care markets. NBER Working Paper 12301. Cambridge, MA: National Bureau of Economic Research.

General Medical Council. 2006. *Duties of a Doctor*. London: General Medical Council.

Gibbons, S., and S. Machin. 2005. Paying for primary schools: supply constraints, popularity or congestion. Paper Presented to the Royal Economic Society Annual Conference, University of Nottingham.

Gibbons, S., and O. Silva. 2006. *Faith Primary Schools: Better Schools or Better Pupils?* London: Centre for Economic Performance, London School of Economics and Political Science.

Gibbons, S., S. Machin and O. Silva. 2006. *Competition, Choice and Pupil Achievement*. London: Centre for the Economics of Education, London School of Economics and Political Science.

Glasby, J. Forthcoming. *Understanding Health and Social Care*. Bristol: Policy Press.

Glasby, J., and F. Hasler. 2004. A healthy option? Direct payments and the implications for health care. Discussion Document, National Centre for Independent Living and the University of Birmingham Health Service Management Centre.

Glasby, J., and R. Littlechild. 2002. *Social Work and Direct Payments*. Bristol: Policy Press.

Glendinning, C., S. Halliwell, S. Jacobs, K. Rummery and J. Tyrer. 2000. Bridging the gap: using direct payments to purchase integrated care. *Health and Social Care in the Community* 8:192–200.

Goodwin, N. 1998. GP fund-holding. In *Learning from the NHS Internal Market* (ed. J. Le Grand, N. Mays and J.-A. Mulligan). London: Kings Fund.

Gorard, S., J. Fitz and C. Taylor. 2003. *Schools, Markets and Choice Policies*. London: RoutledgeFalmer.

Greene, J. P., and M. A. Winters. 2004. Competition passes the test. *Education Next* 4:66–71.

Hannah, G., C. Dey and D. Power. 2006. Trust and distrust in network-style organisation: GPs' experiences and views of a Scottish local healthcare co-operative. *Accounting Forum* 30:377–88.

Hasler, F. 2003. *Clarifying the Evidence on Direct Payments into Practice*. London: National Centre for Independent Living (NCIL).

Hauck, K., and A. Street. Forthcoming. Do targets matter? A comparison of English and Welsh national health priorities. *Health Economics*, in press.

Hibbard, J. 2003. Engaging healthcare consumers to improve the quality of care. *Medical Care* 41 (Supplement):I-61–I-70.

Hibbard, J., and E. Peters. 2003. Supporting informed consumer health decisions: data presentation approaches that facilitate the use of information in choice. *Annual Review of Public Health* 24:413–33.

Hirschman, A. 1970. *Exit, Voice and Loyalty*. Cambridge, MA: Havard University Press.

House of Commons Public Administration Select Committee. 2005. *Choice, Voice and Public Services* (HC 49-1). London: TSO.

Hoxby, C. M. 1994. Do private schools provide competition for public schools? NBER Working Paper 4978, National Bureau of Economic Research, Cambridge MA.

———. 2002. How school choice affects the achievement of public school students. In *Choice with Equity* (ed. P. Hill). Stanford, CA: Hoover Press.

———. 2003. School choice and school productivity (or, is school choice a rising tide that lifts all boats?). In *The Economic Analysis of School Choice* (ed. C. M. Hoxby). University of Chicago Press.

———. 2005. Competition among public schools: a reply to Rothstein (2005). NBER Working Paper 11216, National Bureau of Economic Research, Cambridge, MA.

Hughes-Hallet, T. 2005. At home, with cats, kids and morphine. *The Guardian*, July 7.

Joseph, C., H. Lowry, J. Rafferty, S. Barber and V. Dseagu. 2006. *Supporting Patient Choice: Learning from Stakeholders*. Manchester: NHS Northwest Strategic Health Authority and the Council for Ethnic Minority Voluntary Sector Organisations.

Joseph Rowntree Foundation. 2004. *Making Direct Payments Work for Older People*. York: Joseph Rowntree Foundation.

Kennedy, A., C. Gately, A. Rogers and the EPP Evaluation Team. 2005. *Process Evaluation of the EPP Report II: Examination of the Implementation of the Expert Patients Programme within the Structure and Locality Contexts of the NHS in England (PREPP Study)*. Manchester: National Primary Care Research and Development Centre.

Klein, R. 2005. The great transformation. *Health Economics, Policy and Law* 1:91–98 (reprinted in the 2006 paperback edition of Le Grand (2003)).

Lamont, E., D. Hayreh, K. Pickett, J. Dignam, M. List, K. Stenson, D. Harat, B. Brockstein, S. Sellargren and E. Vokes. 2003. Is patient travel distance associated with survival on phase II clinical trials in oncology? *Journal of the National Cancer Institute* 95:1370–75.

Lauder, H., and D. Hughes. 1999. *Trading in Futures: Why Markets in Education Don't Work*. Philadelphia, PA: Open University Press.

Leece, J., and J. Bornat (eds). 2006. *Developments in Direct Payments*. Bristol: The Policy Press.

Le Grand, J. 1984. Equity as an economic objective. *Journal of Applied Philosophy* 1:39–51.

——. 1989. Markets, equality and welfare. In *Market Socialism* (ed. J. Le Grand and S. Estrin). Oxford University Press.

——. 1991. *Equity and Choice: An Essay in Economics and Applied Philosophy*. London: Harper Collins Academic.

——. 2002. The Labour Government and the National Health Service. *Oxford Review of Economic Policy* 18:137–53.

——. 2003. *Motivation, Agency and Public Policy: Of Knights and Knaves, Pawns and Queens*. Oxford University Press (paperback edition published in 2006).

Le Grand, J., and W. Bartlett (eds). 1993. *Quasi-Markets and Social Policy*. Houndmills: Macmillan.

Le Grand, J., N. Mays and J.-A. Mulligan (eds). 1998. *Learning from the Internal Market: A Review of the Evidence*. London: Kings Fund.

Lent, A., and N. Arend. 2004. *Making Choices: How Can Choice Improve Local Public Services?* London: New Local Government Network.

Levačić, R. 2004. Competition and the performance of English secondary schools: further evidence. *Education Economics* 12:177–93.

Levett, R., with I. Christie, M. Jacobs and R. Therivel. 2003. *A Better Choice of Choice.* London: Fabian Society.

Lewis, R., A. Alvarez-Rosete and N. Mays. 2006. *How to Regulate Health Care in England: An International Perspective.* London: Kings Fund

Lipsey, D. 2005. Too much choice. *Prospect* 117 (December).

Machin, S., and S. McNally. 2004. *The Literacy Hour.* London: Centre for the Economics of Education.

Marquand, D. 2004. *Decline of the Public: The Hollowing Out of Citizenship.* Cambridge: Polity Press.

Marshall, M., P. Shekelle, S. Leatherman and R. Brook. 2000. The public release of performance data. What do we expect to gain? A review of the evidence. *Journal of the American Medical Association* 283:1866–74.

Martikainen, T., and S. Frediksson. 2006. Vaalit ja politiikka ['Elections and politics']. City of Helsinki, Urban Facts. Research Publications 5/2006. Helsinki.

Mayer, R., J. Davis and F. Schoorman. 1995. An integrative model of organizational trust. *Academy of Management Review* 20:709–34.

Milligan, C., C. Woodcock and A. Burton. 2006. *Turning Medicaid Beneficiaries into Purchasers for Health Care: Critical Success Factors for Medicaid Consumer-Directed Purchasing.* Washington, DC: Academy Health.

MORI. 2005. Survey of 2000 adults in Great Britain 18+. London: IPSOS MORI.

National Birthday Trust. 1997. *Home Births—The Report of the 1994 Confidential Enquiry.* Carnforth: Parthenon.

NHS Confederation. 2003. *Fair for All, Personal to You: The NHS Confederation Response to the Choice Consultation*. London: NHS Confederation.

Noden, P., A. West, M. David and A. Edge. 1998. Choices and destinations at transfer to secondary schools in London. *Journal of Education Policy* 13:221–36.

O'Shaughnessy, J., and C. Leslie. 2005. *More Good School Places*. London: Policy Exchange.

Page, B.. 2004. The impact on public expectation. In *Patient Power: The Impact of Patient Choice on the Future NHS* (ed. M. Mythen and T. Coffey). London: New Health Network.

Palmer, K. 2005. *How Should We Deal with Hospital Failure: Facing the Challenges of the New NHS Market*. London: Kings Fund.

Pfizer/MORI Health Choice Index. 2005. Public opinion on choice in out of hospital care (December 2005; see www.ipsos-mori.com/polls/2005/pdf/hci051028.pdf).

Pinker, R. 1971. *Social Theory and Social Policy*. London: Heinemann.

———. 1979. *The Idea of Welfare*. London: Heinemann.

———. 2006. From gift relationships to public policy: an odyssey along the policy paths of altruism and egoism. *Social Policy and Administration* 40:10–25 (reprinted in the 2006 paperback edition of Le Grand (2003)).

Pollock, A. 2005. *NHS plc: The Privatisation of Our Health Care*. London: Verso.

Porter, M., and E. Teisberg. 2006. *Redefining Health Care: Creating Value-Based Competition on Results*. Boston, MA: Harvard Business School Press.

Prabhakar, R. 2006. *Rethinking Public Services*. Houndmills: Palgrave Macmillan.

Preker, A., and A. Harding. 2002. *Innovations in Health Service Delivery: The Corporatization of Public Hospitals*. Washington, DC: World Bank Publications.

Prime Minister's Strategy Unit (PMSU). 2005. *Improving the Life Chances of Disabled People*. London: PMSU.

Prime Minister's Strategy Unit (PMSU). 2006a. *School Reform: A Survey of Recent International Experience*. London: PMSU.

———. 2006b. The UK government's approach to public service reform. Discussion paper, PMSU.

Propper, C., S. Burgess and K. Green. 2004. Does competition between hospitals improve the quality of care? Hospital death rates and the NHS internal market. *Journal of Public Economics* 88:1247–72.

Propper, C., D. Wilson and S. Burgess. 2006. Extending choice in English health care: the implications of the economic evidence. *Journal of Social Policy* 35:537–57.

Raham, H. 2002. *Decentralization and Choice in Sweden's School System: Policy Lessons for Canada*. Kelowna, BC: Society for the Advancement of Excellence in Education.

Rankin, J. 2005. A good choice for mental health. Mental Health in the Mainstream, Working Paper 3, Institute for Public Policy Research, London.

Rothstein, J. 2005. Does competition among public schools benefit students and taxpayers? A comment on Hoxby. NBER Working Paper 11,215, National Bureau of Economic Research, Cambridge, MA.

Scheffler, R. 1989. Adverse selection: the Achilles heel of the NHS reforms. *The Lancet* 1:950–52.

Schultze, C. 1977. *The Private Use of Public Interest*. Washington, DC: Brookings Institution.

Schwappach, D., and C. Koeck. 2004. Preferences for disclosure: the case of bedside rationing. *Social Science and Medicine* 59:1891–97.

Schwartz, B. 2004. *The Paradox of Choice: Why More is Less*. New York: HarperCollins.

Smith, A. 1776/1964. *The Wealth of Nations*, Everyman's Library. London: Dent.

Söderström, M., and R. Uusitalo. 2005. School choice and segregation: evidence from an admissions reform. Working Paper 2005:7, Institute for Labour Market Policy Evaluation (IFAU) (see www.ifau.se / upload / pdf / se / 2005 / wp05-07.pdf, accessed 28 September 2006).

Spiers, J. 2003. *Patients, Power and Responsibility*. Abingdon: Radcliffe Medical Press.

Stevens, S. 2004. Reform strategies for the English NHS. *Health Affairs* 23:37–44.

Sutton Trust. 2005. *No More School Run*. London: Social Market Foundation, Policy Exchange, Sutton Trust.

Swedish National Agency of Education. 2003. School choice and its effects in Sweden: a summary. Report 230, Lenanders Grafiska AB, Kalmar.

Taylor, D. 2004. *Valuing Choice: Dying at Home*. London: Marie Curie Cancer Care.

Thomas, S., and R. Oates. 2005. *The Parent Factor Report Four: Access to Education*. Auckland: The Maxim Institute.

Titmuss, R. 1997. *The Gift Relationship* (new edition edited by A. Oakley and J. Ashton). London School of Economics. (First edition published in 1970.)

Tomkins, C. 2001. Interdependencies, trust and information in relationships, alliances and networks. *Accounting Organisations and Society* 26:161–91.

Turner, G.-M. 2005. *Consumerism in Health Care: Early Evidence Is Positive*. Alexandra, VA: The Galen Institute.

Van Beusekon, I., S. Tonshoff, H. De Vries, C. Spreng and E. B. Keeler. 2004. *Possibility or Utopia? Consumer Choice in Health Care: A Literature Review*. Santa Monica, CA: RAND.

Vickers, J., and G. Yarrow. 1988. *Privatization: An Economic Analysis*. Cambridge, MA: MIT Press.

Waslander, S., and M. Thrupp. 1995. Choice, competition and segregation: an empirical analysis of a New Zealand secondary education market 1990–1993. *Journal of Education Policy* 10:1–26.

Weale, A. 1983. *Political Theory and Social Policy*. London: Macmillan.

West, A., and A. Hind. Forthcoming. School choice in London, England: characteristics of students in different types of schools. *Peabody Journal of Education*, in press.

West, A., and H. Pennell. 2003. *Underachievement in Schools*. London: RoutledgeFalmer.

West, A., A. Hind and H. Pennell. 2004. School admissions and 'selection' in comprehensive schools: policy and practice. *Oxford Review of Education* 30:347–69.

Which? 2005. Choice: can the government's choice agenda deliver for consumers (see www.which.co.uk/files/application/pdf/0503choice_rep-445-55216.pdf, accessed 28 September 2006).

Williams, J., and A. Rossiter (eds). 2004. *Choice: The Evidence*. London: Social Market Foundation.

Witcher, S., K. Stalker, M. Roadburg and C. Jones. 2000. Direct payments; the impact on choice and control for disabled people. Central Research Unit, Scottish Executive (see www.scotland.gov.uk/cru/documents/dpdp-00.asp, accessed 28 September 2006).

Witte, J. 1997. Achievement effects of the Milwaukee Public School Voucher Program. Paper presented to *The American Economics Association Annual Meeting, 3–6 January 1997* (see http://dpls.dacc.wisc.edu/choice/aea97.html, accessed 28 September 2006).

Wood, C. 2005. *Making Choice a Reality in Secondary Education*. London: Social Market Foundation.